745.5922
Oro
c 1

ELMHURST PUBLIC LIBRARY

3 1135 00619 9951

P9-CQV-561

DESIGNING *the* DOLL

FROM CONCEPT TO CONSTRUCTION

SUSANNA OROYAN

C&T PUBLISHING

ELMHURST PUBLIC LIBRARY
ELMHURST, IL 60126

Copyright © 1999 by Susanna Oroyan
Editor: Cyndy Lyle Rymer
Technical Editor: Sara Kate MacFarland
Book Design: Christina Jarumay
Cover Design: Christina Jarumay
Illustrator: Thomas Oroyan
Front Cover Photographs: (clockwise from top left):
Child of the Depression by Susan Fosnot, 20", oil painted cloth doll. Photo by Ann P. Nevills
Zelda by Donna Beacock, 21", cloth. Photo by Sandra Hoover
Yakuza's Butterfly by Robin Foley, 16", sculpted cloth, Japanese silk. Photo by W. Donald Smith
Blue and Orange Abstracts by Susanna Oroyan, 15" and 12". Photo by W. Donald Smith
The Prioress Eglantine by Sandra Wright Justiss, 22", paperclay. Photo by W. Donald Smith
Aileshia by Gillie Charleson; 36", porcelain and cloth. Photo by Gillie and John Charleson
They, Them & Us by Janet Kay Skeen, 12"-13", cotton, paint and beads. Photo by Ken Sanville
Untitled by Pamela Cowart Rickman, 18", cotton muslin, colored pencils, acrylics, paperclay. Photo by Richard Dorbin
Roland Montague by Chris Chomick and Peter Meder; 21", Cernit. Photo by Chris Chomick
Back Cover Photograph: Nonesuch by Bill Nelson and Tom Banwell, 18", resin and mixed media. Photo by Dennis McWaters
Title Page Photograph: Dancing by Akiko Sasaki, 16", cloth. Photo by Akiko Sasaki

The copyrights on individual works are retained by the artists. The drawings and written instructional material are under copyright and may not be reproduced for any purpose without permission of the artist and author. Dolls or parts of dolls shown in photographic illustrations should be considered under copyright to the individual creator.

All rights reserved. No part of this work covered by the copyright hereon may be reproduced or used in any form or by any means—graphic, electronic, or mechanical, including photocopying, recording, taping, or information storage and retrieval system—without written permission of the publisher.

We take great care to ensure that the information included in this book is accurate and presented in good faith, but no warranty is provided nor results guaranteed. Since we have no control over the choice of materials or procedures used, neither the author nor C&T Publishing, Inc. shall have any liability to any person or entity with respect to any loss or damage caused directly or indirectly by the information contained in this book.

Attention Teachers: While you may not copy any portion of the work as stated above, C&T Publishing encourages you to use this book as a text for teaching. Contact us at www.ctpub.com for information about selected lesson plans for our titles.

Celastic is a registered trademark of Degussa AG
Celluclay is a registered trademark of Activa Products, Inc.
Cernit is a registered trademark of T & F Kunstafee Fur Technik und Freizeit GMBH
Claymation is a registered trademark of Will Vinton Productions, Inc.
Corian is a registered trademark of E.I. Du Pont de Nemours and Company.
Creative Paperclay is a registered trademark of Creative Paperclay Company, Inc.
Fimo is a registered trademark of Eberhard Faber, Germany
Fome-Cor is a registered trademark of Monsanto Company, Delaware Corporation
Kerr Syringe Elasticon is a registered trademark of Detroit Dental Manufacturing Company
LaDoll is a brand name of Padico
Lycra is a registered trademark of E.I. DuPont de Nemours and Company
Pyrex is a registered trademark of Corning Incorporated
Sculpey and Super Sculpey are registered trademarks of Polyform Products
Styrofoam Brand Insulation is a registered trademark of Dow Chemical
Ultrasuede is a registered trademark of Springs Industries, Inc.
Velcro is a registered trademark of Velcro Industries B.V.

Library of Congress Cataloging-in-Publication Data
Oroyan, Susanna.
    Designing the Doll : from concept to construction / Susanna
Oroyan.
       p.   cm.
   Includes bibliographical references and index.
   ISBN 1-57120-060-6
   1. Dollmaking.   I. Title
TT175.07598 1999
745.592'21—dc21   98-30312
                                    CIP

Published by C&T Publishing, Inc.
P.O. Box 1456
Lafayette, California 94549

Printed in Hong Kong
10 9 8 7 6 5 4 3 2

Thanks

It takes a team to make a book.

Once again, my thanks to the 130 artists who stopped work to find photos, to fill out forms, and to share information.

And once again my thanks and appreciation to the editors and staff of C&T Publishing who welcome me to their team in working to put the photos, drawings, and text into the best possible presentation of my ideas. It is a joy to work with such caring professionals.

And, as always my love and thanks to Tom who makes my sketches into drawings which communicate with clarity and delight...and who really makes all of it possible.

Gertrude Van Whysse by Susanna Oroyan.
Photo by W. Don Smith

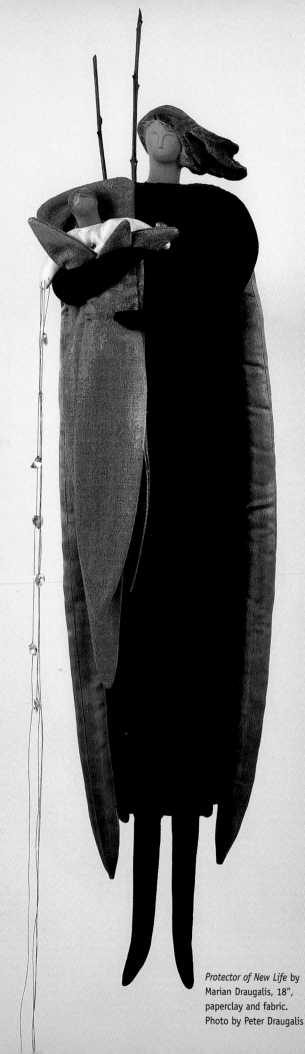

Protector of New Life by
Marian Draugalis, 18",
paperclay and fabric.
Photo by Peter Draugalis

Contents

Learning the Way by Marian Draugalis, 28", paperclay and fabric. Photo by Peter Draugalis

Preface

Dollmaker: Where Do You Get the Heads?
by Susanna Oroyan, 15", paperclay over
wire armature. Photo by W. Don Smith

This book is for those who said, "I don't know what those things are, but I want to make them. Show me how to do it or show me how to do it better."

I am not sure what these things are myself, and I have been making them for a long time. Sometimes what I do is fine art—abstract, realistic, or impressionistic figure sculpture. Sometimes what I do is commercial toy design. Sometimes, it's dimensional illustration. Those who speak English tend to lump all of these forms under the word "doll," as I have in the title of this book. However, a more adequate description of those things we make might be figurative sculpture. We take raw materials and an idea, and combine them to make a figure that represents some aspect of the human condition. It might be something that a child could play with, it might be a mechanical store window display, or it might be a figure that represents a favorite literary character.

Like me, you make these figures or want to because you are interested in people, mechanics, and materials. And you enjoy creating challenges for yourself or problems to solve. That's where this book comes in. I try to provide some ways to show you how to go about the designing or problem solving that might make things go faster or smoother for you.

Why would I and other doll artists want to do this? Because nothing can compare to the joy you feel when you have successfully completed an original piece of art. If we can help make that possible for others, we want to do it. Also, we are just plain doll "junkies." We want to see more and we want to see different and we want to see better.

If I had to put the answer to how to make figures in one sentence it would be: "Just do it and think about what you are doing." Thinking about it involves getting hold of an idea or a visualization of what you want to do and then figuring out what problems you have to solve to get there. For all of us whose work you see in this book, the thinking about it, the doing it, the getting there is the fun part. It's why when we finish one, we go on to do another, and another, and another....

Those of us who are interested in figure making are pretty much visually oriented hands-on people. We like studying human activities, emotions, and shapes. We like the textures of fabric and the colors of paint. We get great satisfaction from putting things together so they work well.

We look at pictures of figures first. Usually, when we read about figures, it's to find out more about the pictures. We want to know what happened to get what we see in the pictures. Outside of our own hands-on, brains-on experiences, that's really how we learn.

I have pictures and I have drawings I can show you. I can tell you about the pictures. But the "what happened" part has to do with thinking. How this artist got those wings or how that artist made the figure stand on one tip-toe is the result of how each one thought out the problem. Artists can't put the materials together to get the effect until they think out how they will do it. This thinking out is a pretty jumpy business. It jumps between ideas, techniques, and materials. It explores and rejects several solutions before picking the right one for the particular piece. It has to have back-up information or experience to know when a solution won't work.

It's pretty hard to show a series of thought processes, especially when those processes are pretty much nonverbal and almost never flow in a logical, sequential fashion. Books have to have "flow." Books have to make sense as whole works of design themselves. The easiest kind of solution to the book as a design problem is to present individual how-to-make-this-doll experiences—essentially patterns where the thinking has been done already. Working through other patterns is good experience, but if you want to make your own original pieces, you don't want to spend too much time doing copy work.

Now, my job is to tell you how to think, or, better yet, how to understand and augment your thinking about figure making.

When we make these pieces we often have the feeling the thing is just appearing under our hands, and that the "I" of us is not really connected to the process. The doing part is spatial; it is manipulating objects. It isn't usually a

Dollmaker: Getting Ideas by Susanna Oroyan, 20", paperclay over wire armature. Photo by W. Don Smith

talking thing. If we are doing it right, we aren't thinking "I want," we are responding to what the piece wants us to do for it. Once while talking with a colleague, I pointed out a particularly pleasing set of descending curves in her sculpture from upper back to heel. She was amazed and said she had never seen her form that way, never *thought* about doing them. She had, but not in a conscious, verbal way. She had visualized a picture of the shape of the figure, and then her hands had done what was needed to make that shape happen in clay. She hadn't had a conversation with herself about it. The talking "I" of her was doing secretarial work quietly in the background. It was giving her the bits of technical information, the hints, and the critical input she needed as she worked back and forth with the piece.

The most important element of the thinking part of creating, or the secretarial "I," is consciousness of design, and there are elements of design that must be considered in every creation such as form, texture, balance, proportion. This might seem rather awesome and academic. It might help to think of design as imagineering—you imagine the idea you want to express and you engineer it to bring it into tangible reality. This is the stuff that goes on in your head. Your hands are just doing the work for the instructions your brain has given them (or, to be more precise, what your brain is writing in an on-going manner as you work). The piece and the instructions finish at the same time.

If I were to create a school to teach figure making, I would be providing things for the secretarial "I" to know and access: experiences with using the elements of design, tools, techniques, and materials. I would not teach you how to make Doll101 Fairy in the Woods or Doll102 Baby in a Bunting. I wouldn't care if you ever made a doll in a class. I would care that you got these experiences and thought about how to use them when you needed to make an idea happen. The actual figure becomes the independent thesis project. All the things you know and can learn—and in making figures you can never know too much— need to be accessed when you get that picture in your mind of what you want to make.

Granted, the material that follows will be my particular way of structuring this universe, but not entirely. If they stop to think about what they do, most artists will pretty much agree with the ideas of developing personal style and learning how to apply good design. Most will admit that no matter how well thought-out a project will be, there will always be more problems to solve and some pleasant, unexpected surprises. All will tell you to "just do it," and as you can see, many have shared their ways of making things work.

None of us can tell you how to make your original ideas in a step-by-step fashion, so think of this book as a jumpstart or a review of the major considerations you might encounter when you make a figure.

Fly Away by Beverly Dodge Radefeld, 15", cloth. Photo by W. Don Smith

Lillia and Her Seahorse by Annie Wahl, 6", Super Sculpey. Photo by Lloyd Wilson

Fairy in Flight Training by Sally Lampi, cloth. Photo by Sally Lampi

Swing by Chikako Akune, 35 cm., paperclay face, cloth over wire armature. Photo by Iwao Akune

Funny You Should Ask by elinor peace bailey, 25", cloth. Photo by Isaac Bailey

Introduction

CONSTRUCTIVE THINKING

Craft, dimensional illustration, or fine art; whatever you term what you do, none of the material in this book will help if you do not realize that the idea—in its initial form and through its evolution to the final figure—is the main consideration. Any time you go into the studio, you need

Dollmaker: Heads to Finish by Susanna Oroyan, 18", paperclay over wire armature. Photo by Don Smith

to have an idea of why you are going and what you might want to do there. This book is intended to begin where both *Fantastic Figures* and *Anatomy of a Doll* left off. In both, I spoke to the idea of thinking a doll. Here, we are going to go deeper into the thinking that goes on when we develop a figure from idea to reality.

Figure making, like any other kind of invention, is simply the making of an idea. You have a thought or a concept, and because you feel strongly about wanting to feel and see it you are willing to think more and do extensive handwork to make it become something you can actually hold in your hands.

Thinking a doll involves two different thought modes. The first has to do with the actual how-to-get-it-made processes. This is craft and it is learned by practice and by trial and error. The more you practice and experiment, the better your execution of craft technique will be. The more you know about technique, the more options you have when choosing materials and methods of manipulation. You'll also realize when you need to invent a solution. The body of this book will introduce you to many of the technical processes that are available for figure making.

The second mode involves making design choices. This "choosing" requires imagination and that leads us to art. Art has to do with the personality of the artist, his imaginative capabilities, and his ability to interpret his feelings and his environment. It also has a lot to do with a knowledgable application of the elements of design. It has to do with soul and it has to do with style. It isn't learned, but there is "art" that can be developed in everyone. Before we get to techniques, we need to discuss how design and imagination work together.

The base meaning of imagination is something like "to image"—to be able to visualize an object that does not exist, that has never existed in that form before. We often assign the word the element of creativity. We say someone is imaginative when we mean he is creative because he can think of new ways to put things together. We say he is an artist when he puts those things together in a way that makes a strong impression or causes a strong emotional or intellectual response. What we are looking for in the figure is craft executed to an exciting (new, different) perfection.

Or, rather, a good doll is an exciting thing that is well-engineered.

Let's think about the order/structure of that statement. The subject is the doll-thing and the engineering describes what is being done with that thing. Often, in dollmaking, the emphasis is the other way around. Well-made takes precedence in our minds because it is the part we can get at factually. We can point to loose threads, discuss how to make a joint work well, and teach someone how to use a tool or a machine. But we have big problems talking about our feelings as they appear in a piece or how we feel about another's piece. Yet it is the emotional part that drives the artist and makes his work interesting and appreciated.

In order to develop that creative, imaginative part of your work, the part that uses the technical knowledge, that chooses the materials, you need to begin by thinking a bit about yourself and how you might work best.

Why?

I have to assume you feel that if something is worth doing, it is worth doing well. I assume we all want to make the one-hundred-and-ten percent piece. A few years ago, I looked around at the blossoming world of art figures and thought, "If I could, I would love a collection of all these artist's heads." Oops! Why didn't I want whole figures? Because, if pressed, I would have said that while the heads were excellent, the body sculpture, proportion, or costuming choices were not as well-thought out, not as well-designed, as the idea defined in the sculpted head.

If the head equals ten points, every other part of the design and construction ought to get ten points to make a 100 percent piece. Then the piece needs to be able to get another ten points for "artistic interpretation"—Style, signature, the "wow" factor.

ARE YOU AN IMAGINEER?

Only these very important qualities are required: The first is the ability to be receptive to any and all stimuli that might provide a figure idea. The second is the ability to identify and solve a problem or satisfy a need. The third is a willingness to be experimental or to identify and accept failure and to fix it or drop it. That's all.

First and last, your goal is to communicate an idea or to provoke an emotional or intellectual reaction. In order to get full points for every part and the bonus points, every decision you make, every technique you apply, needs to be bounced off the controlling factor of idea/final result. Some of those extra points are the personal property of the artist going in, and some are the result of a final adjustment. Some, maybe more than we think, are assigned along the way as the artist fine-tunes his vision with considerations and applications of technique.

The type and nature of your ideas, which are your personal property, will direct the outcome of your work. In the world of the figure maker we have endless idea potential. Some of these are quite complex and some very basic. Ideas equate to figures in a relationship something like this:

- *Figure/idea that has no purpose: pure personal artistic expression = a fine art figure*
- *Figure/idea that suggests purpose: looks like, but is not, an art figure in play doll form = dimensional illustration*
- *Figure/idea that has purpose: it does something or is something = play doll, an advertising figure, or a fashion mannequin*

The fine art figure can take any form with any material, and its concept and execution are totally directed by the artist. The idea or suggestion for the purposeful piece often comes from an external source (a client, a design challenge), and the artist's job is to tool his ideas so the purpose is achieved well. The middle area is the one that causes problems in the idea department. It is also the biggest area of figure making—making dolls for collectors who like things that look like evolved play dolls or dimensional illustration. The artist's job is usually figuring out the market taste. Quite often, the market is not as demanding as the client or as accepting as the art collector. In this case the maker can focus by either forgetting the selling part and creating art, becoming his own client, or identifying a client type closest to his natural inclinations and tailoring his thinking accordingly.

Most people, including the makers themselves, tend to think of making original pieces as the actual hands-on sculpture and construction process. It involves taking materials and doing something to them to create a form. It's like building a house on an empty lot. But, in making the figure, you are the architect. You have an idea about how it will look and how the parts will have to go together for pleasing effect, and you create the plans. You are the engineer who considers the structure needed to make the house or the figure stand. You are the construction crew that actually hammers the nails. And, looping back, you are the architect who anticipates and fixes problems as they occur during construction.

White Lady by Susanna Oroyan, 10" seated. Photo by W. Don Smith

When you stop to think about what you really do when you make a figure, it ought to go something like this:

Stimulus—*something that pops up in your mental or physical environment that makes you think "I could make that," or "I want to make that as a figure," or "I want to use that to make a figure."*

Challenge—*"How would I do that?"*

Research—*poking around in your background store of knowledge to see what things you know that could apply to solving the problem of how. Sometimes this is actual research, sometimes this means learning or figuring out a new method or technique.*

Preliminary design—*"If I do this, then I have to do that to make the idea communicate."*

More research—*finding the things that will put together a rough draft of your idea. Getting the materials and tools for the specific job you outlined for yourself.*

Design—*getting the idea firmly outlined with guide notes either in your head or on paper.*

Execution—*the actual sculpture and costume construction, what most people think of as the making of the piece.*

Design refinement—*changes and re-thinking as you go along. The best laid plans will often not fall together when real materials are constructed. What happens when your work or another stimulus gives you a new idea or a new visualization of the original concept?*

Other considerations—*such as "Will this photograph well? Will this sell in the market? Will the client like it? How could I pack and ship this piece?"*

Design critique—*sitting back and taking a long, hard, non-emotional look at the piece to identify any unsatisfactory areas.*

Work—*making yourself fix or create each part to the best of your ability.*

Design integration—*perhaps the most important part. Making sure all the parts work well together, each one as perfect as it can be, while no one part detracts from or dominates over the whole.*

Completion—*all the things that need to be done after the figure is complete to make it presentable/usable. Stands, tags, packaging.*

Notice there were six steps to be done before you actually picked up the tools and raw materials for the actual execution, and six things to do after the work was roughed in. Of course, if you never execute the idea, it will remain a fuzzy visualization in your head or rough sketches on paper. It won't dimensionally illustrate your thinking or ideas, but—and this is important—every single step is crucial to the completion of the successful piece.

And only two parts are actual hands-on making or manipulating material—the rest is head work: imagineering. Granted, for many of us this head work is done on "auto-think."

Now I want to go back and look at the stimuli. These are the things within you that make the art part. Where do your ideas come from? Are they different from those of others? Do you say, "I like that idea so I think I will make it into a doll?" Or do you say, "There is a shape and a color I like together. How might they become a figure that is uniquely mine?" If you are the type of person who gets what I call prepackaged ideas, then it is fairly likely your work will be immediately recognizable as something or some subject. An example might be "I want to make Little Red Riding Hood or a beautiful ballerina in the Firebird costume." Here some other element—usually a picture or a written description—provides a good deal of the design solution for you. All you have to do is find the parts and put them together—make a little girl in a red hooded cape. Many artists will put an individual interpretive spin on an external idea: make Little Red Riding Hood as motorcycle mama in red leather, for instance.

Another type of idea comes from what I call internal floating fragments. These might be the result of visualizations of color and form that you hook together. They float along for some time until a face or a character idea shows up that seems to go with them. All three of these elements might float along until a fabric shows up that works well with the color hooks. Three or four elements like this hooked and floating are an embryonic idea. Usually, at that point, you start paying attention to it and pushing the elements around to bring the idea into focus a bit better. When the focus is sharpened, then you start thinking about deconstructing the idea in order to do the actual design engineering.

Separation by Emily Owen, 9", paperclay. Photo by Emily Owen

THINKING RE-THOUGHT

The key to making art figures or dolls is having a great deal of knowledge about methods and materials along with an ability to think of the easiest solution for a design challenge. The computer terms for memory—"read only" and "random access"—very much describe what a person needs to have in his head to think a figure into reality; you have to scroll through your knowledge of techniques and available materials.

Design is getting, holding, and developing the idea. Success is the ability to know when the idea is good and/or when all parts of it work most efficiently and harmoniously.

YOUR GOALS

If you come from a doll world orientation, ideas in terms of subject matter are provided. Dolls can be fairies, pretty children, grumpy grandpas, or recognizable personalities. All of these are generalized concepts or notions that the doll-appreciating culture of the world can universally identify with. These are safe subjects. If you do them, people know what they are. Your viewer has a built-in judgment gauge when he looks at them. However, his judgment gauge is going to be just a little different from yours and, perhaps, a little more particular. Your job as an artist is to make your interpretation of fairy-ness or Santa-ness just a little sharper and more outstanding.

Or, and this is equally as important, your job is to jolt the viewer by breaking up his expectations, by making him think or react to the piece in an emotional or intellectual way. This is usually the case when you create abstract, cartoon, satirical, or emotionally moving pieces. Either way, your job is to make your piece the one that makes an impression on the viewer. Why would you want to do that? Are you doing that? How can you do that?

Stressing the need to make a strong impression or create a reaction might seem a bit much, but I don't think so. The doll world isn't that demanding, because being associated with play, it doesn't require that everything be spelled out in a piece. However, today most serious dollmakers are not making toys. They are making art or thinking that they are making art. What they call art is often illustration. Even so, both require design and a bit of the "wow" factor.

There is nothing wrong with being an illustrator. Norman Rockwell was a great illustrator. With a highly recognizable style, and incredible abilities in composition and rendering, he reminded us of everyday views and feelings. The only thing that divides the work of a Rockwell from a first-rate doll artist is the element of dimension. I am and have been a dimensional illustrator. For many years I was very uncomfortable when people referred to me as an artist. Most of my work dealt with characters that were immediately identifiable in our culture. Primarily, they were fairy tale and story book characters or people and scenes from daily life. What I was doing was no more and no less than making a three-dimensional book illustration. The art—my style—appeared only insofar as I modeled the clay, chose odd materials, and put a twist on the interpretation. I had the things required, but not in the right order and not in the right emphasis. I got comfortable with the term artist only when the idea with the maximum twist, not the identifiable subject, became the starting point and governing factor of my design thinking.

Bernice by Jane Darin, 18", cloth. Photo by Werner Kalber. Illustration reprinted from *Trupp* by Janell Cannon, ©1995 by Jannell Cannon. Reproduced by permission of Harcourt Brace & Co. All rights reserved. The doll artist did this dimensional piece as a commission for the author/graphic illustrator.

My example, although true, is a bit extreme. However, its key concept is prioritizing and attitude adjustment. Not all of us go willingly into tidy little boxes. Happiness and success might have a good deal to do with knowing where your work fits. Think about who you are, what you are doing, and where you want to be. Whatever you decide, the element of style and uniqueness in your initial idea should be the first thing you think about when you start to make the figure.

8th Empress-Time by Susanna Oroyan, 20", Super Sculpey. Photo by W. Don Smith This is a piece that came together from floating fragments—a head sculpted as a class example and a chance encounter with a necklace and a pocket watch filed in the "stuff" drawer. Laying the necklace over the head created an "artful accident," along with the challenge of how to make it stay upright in a fixed position.

YOU IN YOUR DOLL

All dollmakers project their personalities into their figures. With some, it's physical—"Jane looks just like her dolls." More likely Jane makes dolls that look like her. With others it is a mental outlook—"Betty really doesn't like children, and whenever she tries to make them, they all look like little monsters." Mental outlook can also be an expression of the artist's emotional construct he does not expose in ordinary life. For instance, a thin artist with a fear of getting fat may tend to do many full-bodied figures, or to make very tall, elongated figures. With some, it is neither mental or physical, more like the ability to see and understand many variations of character. This explains the nice little grandmotherly looking lady who does outrageous abstract figures. It is what I call the "empath" factor: the ability to think of, understand, and execute a personality concept or a life-situation that might not be within your own experience. Think about what you are happily inclined to do, and realize that to do something different will mean more thought and more work.

All dollmakers project their own interests and experiences into the building of their work. A person with a strong ability in costume design and sewing ability will tend to make figures that have very detailed textile work. A person who does not like to sew will usually create more sculptural bodies on which costuming is minimal. As a teacher, when I introduce a new material I often see this at work in my students. We might begin with the same form, but by the end of the day, each form has been personalized by its maker... and those who cannot personalize, the ones who need to be given an idea, are often quite frustrated.

KNOW WHAT YOU WANT TO DO AND WHY

I love beautiful ladies, pretty children, and very accurately scaled portrait figures. That love is admittedly tinged with a bit of envy—these are things I know I cannot do well naturally. Or, more important, I can't do those things well enough to meet my own standards. Once in a while I will attempt, and sometimes finish, one of those types. I do it for the experience—to see if I can get better. However, I have always been enamored of the avant-garde, the different, interesting mechanics, or the weird juxtaposition of ideas. No matter how I try, even my most traditional pieces will inevitably be just a little out of step.

Twenty years ago characters I did were considered "far-out" by the doll world and "trite" by the art world. At the time, I just had to learn which went where if I wanted to sell or exhibit. Nowadays, the lines between areas are far more relaxed, but they do exist. It might be important to you to think about how much you need to make popular work and then to consider where it will be most accepted.

SERIOUS ATTITUDE ADJUSTMENT

As I have taught and listened to students, I find that there are some very real barriers of fear that get between the maker and making. Let's get them out of the way right now.

The biggest problem is usually fear of failure. You look at this book and get charged up to do the same sort of things—you want to be part of this great group of designers. But you are hesitant. Lots of emotional things are keeping your toe from going into the waters. Am I right? Of course I am. I have been there myself and will be there again many times. We all have a degree of stage fright before starting on something new, even if we have done similar things many times.

Let's consider the meaning of failure. Who defines failure? Your mother? Your friends? Your spouse? No. None of the above. You define failure. What is failure? Something that didn't work out the way you wanted it to. So failure, then, is between you and the object. What is the result of failure? A loss of time and a loss of materials. Who lost those things? You did. Do you care that much? Yes, maybe. Maybe you were taught not to waste time or materials, or maybe others told you waste is bad. Nonsense. It isn't. Write it off to experimentation. If you want to be a designer, the name of the game is experimentation. Time is not wasted if you have decided to give yourself that time. Materials are not wasted—you can take apart, change, and re-use. Or, you can agree with yourself that it will take two or three times as much material and time as will actually show in the finished product. Therefore, nothing is really wasted.

Another fear is based on "I can't do that," meaning, "I don't think I am smart enough or skilled enough." Again, who said that? Where did you get that idea? If it came from someone else it is his opinion. It does not have to be yours unless you lie down and let him pin it on you. If it is your idea, then you can fix it by simply banishing the thought. You can learn if you want—though it might take longer. You can teach your hands the skills. People with great physical handicaps have made wonderful figures. Make your excuses challenges.

To say "I can't do that" because you don't have the skills may be true; however, that does not mean you have to take ten classes to learn the technique. Classes should always be taken for experience, never to learn to copy the instructor's method. Try his method and see what parts of it you can use in developing your own approaches. Try what you think the other person did. It won't be the same, but who cares? You would rather do your own thing, right?

If "I can't find the materials" is your problem, then you aren't quite as creative as you need to be. Most of us had no doll-making materials when we started out. Many of us don't need special materials today. We just use whatever is handy. Don't have wig material? Use household string. Don't have fancy fabrics? Use old clothes, use newspapers. Don't have the right striped fabric? Paint the stripes. Don't have a craft store? Use kid's crayons and watercolors from the grocery store or house paint from the hardware store. Being creative means finding solutions in your own environment, using what's on hand. Often these will produce the most interesting results. Like games with rules? OK, make the rule that you must make a doll with things around the house.

Knowing when you have failed is the most important thing for a designer. At that point, you say, "Well, I messed that up." And you do what? Start over. Make another figure that includes improvements in the areas you didn't think were successful. Do another and another.

On the other hand, harder failures happen as a result of the "extraordinary blinding ego." This happens when an artist thinks so well of himself and his work that he cannot critique it himself, take suggestions or help from others, or understand why others' reactions are not enthusiastic.

Now that we have fear under control and realize there are millions of ideas, let's take a look at brains-on design.

Someday I'll Find You by Scott R. Gray, 30", paperclay. Photo by W. Don Smith

UPPER LEFT: *Artemis* by Lisa Lichtenfels, 28", mixed media with nylon skin. Photo by Lisa Lichtenfels

UPPER RIGHT: *Miss Maggie Vernon* by Charles Batte, 16" seated, one-of-a-kind, polymer sculpture, cloth body over wire armature. Photo by Peter Marcus Photography

LOWER RIGHT: *Christina* by Bronwyn Hayes, 30" seated, cloth needlesculpture. Photo by Bronwyn Hayes

UPPER LEFT: *Zoe and Poseidon* by Lily Tolido-Elzer, 13", paperclay head, limbs and fish, cloth over wire armature. Photo by Gerard Tolido

UPPER RIGHT: *Art Deco Inspired Angel* by Van Craig, approx. 25", paperclay/textile with found objects. Commissioned by Richard Simmons for his private collection. Photo by Van Craig

LOWER LEFT: *Untitled (Spring)* by Emily Owen, 15", paperclay. Photo by Emily Owen

UPPER LEFT: *The Loge* by Nancy Wiley, 28", paperclay.
Photo by Robert O'Brien

UPPER RIGHT: *Jacob and Buster* by Diane Keeler, 10", Cernit and
Super Sculpey, cloth and wire armature body. Photo by Lloyd H. Wilson

LOWER RIGHT: *The Girl with the Ball I* by Junko M. Liesfeld,
15", cloth and washi paper. Photo by Jeff Saxman

TOP: *No Joker* by Kathryn Walmsley, 24", Cernit and paperclay, wrapped wire armature. Photo by W. Don Smith

LOWER RIGHT: *Pope John Paul II* by George Stuart, ¼ life-size, mixed media, articulated skeleton, fixed pose, ornaments of precious metal. Photo by Carol Ewing McCartney

UPPER LEFT: *Urban Black Male* by Uta Brauser, 27",
ceramic, posable jointed body. Photo by John Martini

LOWER RIGHT: *Moonlight Shadow* by Jane Davies, 12",
cast porcelain head and hands, wood pulp and wire
armature body. Photo by Jane Davies

UPPER LEFT: *Rapunzel/Hairwashing Day* by Antonette Cely, 18",
paperclay over fabric. Photo by Don B. Cely.

LOWER LEFT: *Miss McLeod* by Barbara Kingman, 14", Super Sculpey.
Photo by David Mathias

UPPER RIGHT: *Sinbad* by Martha Boers and Marianne Reitsma, 18",
Super sculpey over wire armature, cloth body. Photo by Marianne Reitsma

UPPER LEFT: *Granny's Girl* by Diane Keeler, 16", Cernit and Super Sculpey, wire armature and cloth body. Photo by Lloyd H. Wilson

LOWER RIGHT: *Koeki* by Willemijn van der Speigel, 40 cm., impregnated textile. Photo by Ad van den Brink

UPPER LEFT: *Snow White* by Richard St. Clair, 17", paperclay with cloth body. Photo by W. Don Smith

UPPER RIGHT: *Your Muse* by Hennie Koffrie, 16", paperclay, silk, organza, wire frame. Photo by Lauren Janus

LOWER RIGHT: *To Wait* by Elisabeth Flueler-Tomamichel, 9" seated, Sculpey on cloth bodies. Photo by Elisabeth Flueler-Tomamichel

UPPER LEFT: *Torch Song* by Elizabeth Shaw, 19",
Fimo and paperclay over wire armature. Photo by
Elizabeth Shaw

LOWER LEFT: *Tiff* by Retagene Hanslik, 18", Cernit.
Photo by Alan Hanslik

LOWER RIGHT: *White Clown Charles* by Chikako
Akune, wire armature, fabric covered paperclay face.
Photo by Iwao Akune

UPPER LEFT: *Verbonden (Bound Together)* by Willemijn van der Speigel, 42 cm., impregnated textile. Photo by Ad van den Brink

UPPER RIGHT: *What Have They Done With the Card Catalog?* by Elizabeth Brandon, 13", all porcelain, jointed arms. Photo by Berkley Brandon

Making Choices

When you realize you can do whatever you want, it will seem very frightening. All of a sudden there are more possibilities of shape and technical application than you want to deal with. We talked about ideas and getting comfortable with your own expression. Now, you are the person with a vision and you must hold that vision (or drawing) in your mind, when you reach out into this fantastic pile of materials and techniques to pick those that you feel comfortable with and that will make your idea live in the best form.

It gets even more complicated when you find there might be more than one way to illustrate your idea. Or does it? Isn't it more challenging to realize that you could do many versions of the same basic concept? When you realize you could do several variations, the R word (Right) loses it scary power. All you have to do is make your choices right for this piece and any good leftover ideas can be incorporated in another version. This choice making is called design.

PROBLEM SOLVING

Some people are self-directed—they get the idea and all they want is some technical information as to how to make the idea happen. Some people are other-directed—they want to be told how to make it in a step-by-step pattern. A problem occurs when you want very much to make your own designs, but you want someone else to tell you how to do this. That can't be done. No one else can get inside your head and interpret your idea for you. If you want to design, you are going to have to do the instruction writing for yourself. Designing is problem solving, so we start our set of instructions by posing a set of problems—asking and answering a set of questions.

Start with the concept
- *Idea - Who is this figure?*
- *Expression/impression - What is this figure telling us?*
- *Focus - Are there elements of this idea that can be emphasized to help make the point?*
- *Theme motifs - What other elements can be repeated to provide secondary emphasis?*

Add in your type preference
- *Art figure, doll figure, dimensional illustration*

Then think about the elements of design
All of the answers to these questions must reinforce the idea and its expression.
- *Form - What shape do I want this to be?*
- *Scale - What size will the figure be?*

- *Color - What colors will accentuate my idea? Which shades, tones, or hues of those colors will work together?*
- *Texture - How do I want the surfaces to appear— rough, smooth, slick, glossy?*
- *Thematic motifs - What things need to go with the idea to make it clear?*

And then think about construction
- *Mechanics - How does this figure have to be built in order to incorporate all the answers above into an actual figure that will stand, sit or move to suit the desired impression?*
- *Techniques - What type of painting will I use? What type of construction will go with this idea?*

I usually answer these questions in my head. I have often described this process as running a little film or projecting the bits and pieces on the bulletin board of my brain and then moving them around until I get a vision I like. Artist E.J. Taylor says he often imagines the figure as a character on stage. Some people make loose sketches and some make very detailed annotated drawings. The late Robert McKinley, who was a graphic artist, said he tried to avoid a detailed drawing because he felt if he had invested a lot of time in the drawing, he would obligate himself to do the figure exactly as he drew it. But Bob did make rough sketches. Those who can draw well usually think with a pencil. As a verbal person, I have learned to make a very rough sketch and then write a lot of notes—especially if it is an idea I won't be able to do right away. Either way, you have to answer those questions.

The quality of the answers and the choices you make to implement them will be the difference between a good piece and a so-so piece. How you answer will also be a function of how willing you are to be your own tough critic. When you are not sure about the answers, it is a good idea to ask other artists for critical input.

Again, notice that the design process above started with the idea. It did not start with a sculptural material and it did not start with a technical process such as a specific joint. Many people think if they learn enough processes, they will make good figures. As you can see, a person who could do super sculpture or make wonderful joints would not necessarily make a well-designed piece. Classes are great, but the most important ones are those where you learn to make choices and to defend those choices as part of a total design concept. The most important design question you can ask yourself is "Why?" If you can say firmly, "I did that because it works well/doesn't look right with those colors, that texture, that shape, and my idea" then you will be well on your way to making the doll you wanted to make. The most important answer is "no." If you can answer, "no, this won't work," then you are free to explore things that will.

When you have answered the questions above, you have roughed in the basic concept. You can now see what the finished doll figure is going to look like (you hope!).

Your real design work is just beginning. As you work, you will need to address the following issues as you develop your design concept.

Construction

- *Type of material for sculpture*
- *Body surface material - cloth, sculpted material*
- *Body packing/stuffing*
- *Body armatures/body joints*
- *Type of hair material*
- *Type of eye treatment (sculpted)*
- *Type of eye treatment (inset - glass, plastic, other material)*
- *Accessories - scale*

Costume trim and embellishment

- *Color, texture, scale/weight*
- *Costume design cuts and fit - darts, curves, pleats*
- *Costume underpinnings such as hoops, bustles,*

Sculpture

- *Type of material for finished look*
- *Types of materials for original sculpture when finish material is different*
- *Requirements for best use of material and its finishing*
- *Sculpted head (where most think it starts and ends)*
- *Sculpted parts engineered for a cloth or leather body*
- *Sculpted parts engineered for a sculpted body*
- *Making molds for casting sculpted parts*
- *Mold material types*
- *Armatures for making sculpture*
- *The original idea - again, and again, and again*
- *Sketches and/or scaled drawings/templates*

Design variations for the idea

- *Where to obtain materials for all of the above*
- *How to make do when materials aren't available*
- *How to make all kinds of things from shoes to?*
- *How to make this packable/transportable*
- *How to make a piece someone else can set up*
- *How to make the piece as permanent as possible*

And the curve-ball questions

- *It probably isn't good design, but can I get away with it for the "art" of the piece?*

or, rephrased

- *Can I break my own rule/design to make the piece more exciting? How far can I go?*

Empress of Hearts by Susanna Oroyan, 20", polyform. Photo by W. Don Smith

You can break rules. Two wrongs can make a right. And three might really jar the viewer's expectations and drive home the point. Just be sure that if you do choose something different you can justify it in your overall presentation.

We can, and often do, mess up on a design. Rather than trash it, sometimes we can work with the problem. Really creative trouble-shooting can result in some very nice unexpected effects. Don't toss, try again. Re-design it.

All of the items on that long list can be further broken down into two, three, or more subheadings of possibilities to consider! All of these things must be considered at least once in the creation of any figure. Most of them will be covered more than once in a looping fashion. For instance, you might decide to make a sculpted joint, but the material you would like to use won't work well so you have to reconsider. Obviously, the more thinking you can do before you begin actual work, the less down-time will be needed to back out of blind alleys.

Most of us tend to start with the idea for the head. There was a time when I would just pick up clay and doodle until a personality suggested itself. In recent years, I find that the idea is usually a combination of form, color, mechanics, and some notion of personality. Nowadays, I spend considerable time thinking about materials and mechanics before I have a clear realization of the facial portraiture. This type of design is like bringing a blurry image into focus.

PUTTING IT ALL TOGETHER: DESIGNING LUCY

I can make all the lists in the world, but sometimes a real-life example can underline the point. Here is the design process as I applied it to *Lucy I*. Many experienced figure makers will recognize similar steps in their own work.

This one started with "stuff"—things artists pick up to use at some point in the future. I had a pair of translucent, paperweight glass buttons that could have a very startling effect as eyes. The Beatles song title "Lucy in the Sky with Diamonds" kept running through my head....What does she look like? Sparkle and glitter.

I think a bit about how "Lucy" might look. The eyes are clear with a pink rose and a blue swirl and they must be immediately noticeable. Diamonds can be put in the hair. The hair can be coils of metal scrub pad cross-woven with sew-through diamonds in the crossings. The hair needs to start back near the middle or at least very high so as not to detract from the eyes. Sky suggests a backdrop, but I don't want to do more than the figure. Holding lollipops in the same colors as the eyes. Dress something long and floaty, maybe with a bodice of quilted white, a shawl of turquoise that picks up eye color. How to make the figure float "in the sky" on clouds? OK, clouds of what? Stuffing. Stuffing inside clear mylar probably. And then suddenly up pops the idea of a trampoline supported by aluminum or brass rods on a base of black or midnight blue with stars. The dark base will allow me to put a rod up through the center to support the

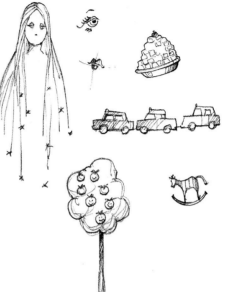

figure so it will appear to float. I could actually run the rod up into a sculpted-to-the-waist torso and let the leg dangle. Who says body has to be a true form? Do what it takes to create the required/desired illusion. I am beginning to "see Lucy." The ideas seem to work and a sketch is made.

Now I listen to the music again and the words and a number of new ideas appear to be considered. Marmalade skies, tangerine trees, cellophane flowers. All of a sudden there is a wholly different figure. Now I have three different concepts of Lucy. Which one

should I do? Or should I blend them? The main thing at this point is the figures are do-able mechanically. There may be changes as I go.

You can see how "messy" design can be in its initial stages. Now we refine. Watch how it changes.

The first thing I did was sculpt a head, but when I inserted the glass buttons for eyes, they did not pick up the light enough to make the necessary kaleidoscope emphasis. I thought about what I could do to make them more translucent—like drill a skylight in her head! I set the whole thing aside. Some time later I experimented with making eyes of polymer clay. I dropped a pair into her head and, *voila!* Not translucent, but the slightly crazy look I wanted. The eyes were going to be the controlling factor—everything had to work with them.

I experimented with tree construction and the design of a base and background that would incorporate other elements of the song lyrics. I spent considerable money on materials as well. I went back to work on the sculpture after deciding I would not have her hold anything in her hand—I wanted the hands to support, but not detract from, the eyes. I wanted them to show tension in an upward direction. I still wanted to have her head in the clouds so I sculpted the head and shoulders as one piece. At this point I had to stop and think about the body design. Again, with the eyes in control, I decided that her costume had to be very simple and cloud-like. This meant I could assemble the parts on a wire armature and cloth-stuffed body.

Before I could begin sculpting the feet I had to design the entire shoe. The shoes could pick up the eye color and reflect the high-heeled wedge style of the 1960s. I also had to decide how the figure would stand—external support rod or pegged into a base. Since heels are fairly small and potentially fragile, I opted for the external support.

When the legs were sculpted, I was faced with an optical illusion problem in the proportioning. This is not uncommon—the high-heeled foot foreshortens. Could I get away with it? Yes, probably. One way was to engineer the figure so the viewer's eye would be drawn upwards by widening the figure at the top and making it narrow as the eye descended. This meant that all the elements I added from this point on had to enforce the idea of upward-ness just as if they were directional arrows.

The upward motion of the figure's costume would have been best accentuated with a lightweight fabric that had a light stripe that could be used vertically. Alas, no such thing could be found. I therefore chose the lightest fabric—a single layer of cheesecloth. Lightness and verticality were again emphasized with the use of very fine silver metallic thread to suspend the "diamonds" from the cloud construction. I could have used clear nylon thread, but I needed the extra hint or direction given by a visible thread.

Now a mechanical real-world problem rears its head: Another design element to keep in mind is wear. I had to capture the clouds in the lightest way possible. This was achieved by stuffing sheer silver and nylon stocking fabric into puffs with silver backing. The puffs were sewn to a silver-covered cardboard base—all her clouds have silver lining!

The slightly "mad" look in the eyes was achieved by creating polyform clay eyes with orange swirls, highlighted with glitter. The effect was further enhanced by several coats of high-gloss laquer.

The head-dress was a serendipity—I happened to see a twist of silver wire on the floor of my studio. When I set it on the head it worked quite well, again providing upward direction. If I had used unraveled scrubpad wire for hair, the upward motion would have been stopped just as if her head had hit a ceiling. Instead of hair, I covered her head with a cap of sheer silver stocking that would suggest a space helmet. The head-dress had to be detachable so it could be packed for travel and shipping—always a design consideration.

The high-heeled feet tend to look small although they measure out proportionally to the full scale of the figure. This problem became a plus as I was more interested in focusing interest on upward movement and the top of the figure.

The final solution for this version is a far cry from the initial possibilities. My process might seem a bit more stream-of-conscious, but notice I considered and answered almost every question in the long list of design elements.

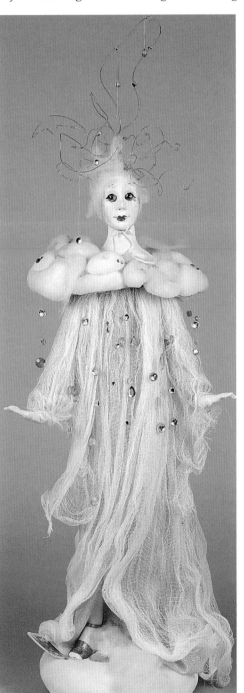

Sticking to a controlling image, in this case the eyes, organized a number of elements. What it means is that I still have many other ways to show Lucy in the Sky with Diamonds—and some expensive stuff to do them with! In this piece, I recognized my own personal inclinations by going monochromatic. For me, the polychromatic version with everything in it would have been far more difficult to organize, and perhaps never as pleasing.

The song is a piece of poetry that for a certain generation sparks instant images and associations. Through my interpretation of the song I am recreating it in another dimension; I'm making the poem a visible thing. By examining the meanings and definitions, and creating a dimensional illustration, I am trying to make a real world version of a hallucination. If it was my hallucination (another word for visualization or idea) then it would be original. These pieces are not wholly original insofar as I have based my art on the interpretation of another art form—fairly common phenomenon in figure making as, for instance, the same as Michaelangelo illustrating the story of Creation in paint on the Sistine Chapel. A person of my generation is likely to make the associational jump when they see Lucy. A younger or older person may not. Question is: A hundred years from now, will there be enough in the piece that, without the name, a person will play with the ideas portrayed?

To review the design:

- *Idea - initial concept of "Lucy in the Sky with Diamonds"*
- *Theme/motif - diamonds, clouds*
- *Focal point - the eyes looking upward*
- *Form - human female, youthful, character*
- *Shape - kite-like/triangulated upward*
- *Line - upward*
- *Color - eyes that were blue, green, orange, blue eyeshadow*
- *Texture - light/fluffy*

Lucy 1 by Susanna Oroyan, 22", paperclay.
Photo by W. Don Smith

Considerations of Form

The point of the "Lucy" example was that at some time during the creation of a figure, the artist attempts to formulate a system that will help him or her present meaning. The more thoughtful the choices, and the more carefully constructed that system is, the better impact the piece will have.

I don't have an art background, so how can I talk about design choices and systems? In my Life Before Dolls, I studied English language and literature. The object of that study was to understand what happens in a piece of literature or in spoken language that makes it communicate well. What we find is that in literature and in art, the more impressive pieces contain highly complex structures that reflect the style or persona of the individual creator. A poem can have end rhyme, or an identifiable interior sound structure—interplay of vowels and consonants—falling and rising pitch and rhythmic beat, or all of those elements. The poet can also communicate his idea with devices such as metaphor, simile, or irony. Looking for these elements requires learning to do heavy-duty structural analysis, and the terms used for doing that in language are the same terms used for the fine arts. I look for texture in the sound of a piece of literature. I look for tactile texture in the visual appearance of the surface of a piece of art.

While a writer might use words to convey colors, an artist would use fabrics. A writer might proportion his work to have a long introduction, a brisk climax, and a short conclusion. An artist might proportion his figure with long legs, a short body, and a big head.

The key thing is that as the artist, you will need to pick or create a system, make sure all of the elements of that system work smoothly together, be able to defend your choices, and defend them when they are something the audience would not normally expect. It might be helpful to think of the system or organization as the world that the figure lives in. All the things that are done in, for, and to the figure have to look like they belong to the figure and its world. The viewer should be able to imagine a world behind it. The tricky part is that you have to create that believable world.

Readers of this book are more likely to be hands-on and dimensionally oriented than interested in or able to do flat art. Many will have attempted either hard or soft sculpture on their own with a book or without benefit of class instruction. The result of this is maybe a good head, a nice pair of hands, some legs, and no idea in the world of how to put them together for good effect. The key is *for good effect*, and that requires working on and thinking about the whole form and its design from the start of the work, not as an afterthought to making pieces or separate parts.

The following are the basic types or forms a figure can take. Choosing one is the first step in building an organizational system for your figure.

Grayces by Susanna Oroyan, 15", paperclay. Photo by W. Don Smith. This piece was organized around several factors: elongated form, tiny roundish skull shapes, simplified, but fairly realistic small hands and feet. Sometimes colors are chosen for their emotional content. In this case, I chose to use grays because I did not want a multicolored figure to distract from the form. I decidedly wanted the gray scape to leave an empty set for the viewer to fill with his own ideas.

TYPE OR FORM

What type of doll does your idea require? What form will it take?

In making figures, or dolls, there are four basic types of form: the realistic human, the toy, the exaggerated or caricature, and the abstract. There are rules or acceptance requirements for all four types. Doll proportion comes from traditional toy design and realistic proportion is based on an average of human anatomical features. Exaggerated or caricatured forms happen when a selected part or set of parts is emphasized. Abstract systems are invented but systematically structured by the artist in a way that allows a communicable impression of realistic form. The type of doll to make will usually appear to you as part of your original concept. However, as you sketch in your character, you need to keep yourself on the right track for selecting the elements of form your figure will require.

What happens if you don't? My first doll, an attempt to show Betsy Ross sewing the American flag, consisted of a sculpted head on a breastplate, arms and legs assembled on a stuffed cloth body. The result was that even though I had sculpted the hand to hold the needle, the arms could not be posed to show the action of sewing. My theme and the attempted refined lady sculpture required the firmly fixed pose of full sculpture or wire armature. My choice of body type failed to create the impact I needed. I also made some poor choices with regard to hair and scale of fabrics. Additionally, I hadn't been making dolls long enough to know that detailed historical figures were not my style. The fact that it was the Bicentennial year was not a good enough reason for me to make this piece. The final result was that the doll was neither fish nor fowl. I hadn't been consistent in creating and following through with one unified system, so the doll wasn't sure if it was a toy doll or an art figure.

Betsy Ross by Susanna Oroyan, 1976, 17", polyform. This bunch of problems is what happens when you make a doll without considering how the elements need to work together. Look and learn and don't let it happen to your work. Photo by W. Don Smith

HUMAN BEGINNINGS

In making figures each type of form has its own set of rules or is given one by the designer. For instance, in making figures of people, whatever we do will have to look like a type of human. The idea might come from any number of places—a vision, photo, incident, or a real person. However, the building of that idea is mental: a visualization, a rough sketch, a pattern, or a direct sculpt begins with the shape—an outline or set of forms. If the shape is not correct, or does not communicate, the figure is doomed from the beginning, no matter how fancy the needlework or how masterful the painting. The figure will not only need to look human-like, but it will have to communicate humanity to the viewer. It will have to be more human-like than dog-like or gorilla-like.

How does a figure tell us that it is a human and not a gorilla? Because it matches (or doesn't match) a mental template of what a human form looks like to us. The form of a gorilla is like a human form, but it varies in the proportion of its shape. The arms are too long, it must be a gorilla/not a human. The head is too forward, must be a gorilla/not a human. Any time you create a human-like figure, you want the viewer to run it by his mental template and say "not a gorilla."

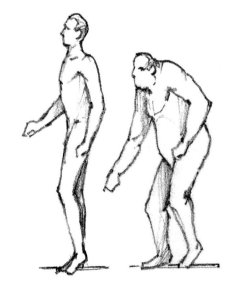

Problems usually crop up when the artist makes a choice to do the human form but does not follow through. Often, both he and the casual viewer will accept a mistake because the human brain defines or identifies on a very forgiving basis. For it to say "human" you only have to show it a few vaguely human parts in relatively the right places. However, when the brain is working in a critical mode, it will require a little more systematically arranged information to say "art" or "nice job." Since we usually want our viewers to like or understand our art, we need to pay some attention to constructing or working with systems to arrange parts.

ANIMAL TYPES

Since many artists who read this might have made animal figures, let's take a moment to discuss identifying differences. Generally, the figure is considered to be a doll or human art figure when the majority of the elements both resemble human body aspects and their placement. For instance, the figure could have the head of a bird, but the head would be placed on a neck implying the head/shoulder construction of the human form. The figure could have this type of a head plus wings and a tail and still be considered essentially human. However, when there are so many animal parts the viewer says "bird," then it is an animal figure and the proportion of the piece is assessed by the comparison to known bird-like characteristics and their possible abstractions. Why do we care? An artist should be comfortable doing what he feels he wants to express, but the world likes to and often needs to categorize. So, the artist needs to be aware that sometimes the blended figure will be rejected or misunderstood when he attempts to place it in a category set by different definitions.

Portrait of Jack at Home by Jo Ellen Trilling, 13", cloth over wire armature. Photo by Jo Ellen Trilling

■ Surprisingly the impact of the figures made by Jo-Ellen Trilling and the late Adnan Karabay come not from their animal aspects, but from the artists' good knowledge of human body proportion. In Karabay's work, the use of human proportion and pose is so well executed the strongest impression is that the figures are indeed human. It takes more mental effort on the part of the viewer to realize he is looking at an animal character. The result for the artist and the viewer is a bonus of enjoyment. In the Trilling work, the effect comes by surprise—the human form is juxtaposed with the totally unexpected addition of a very dog-like head. Here the viewer is given a choice: Is he looking at a dog in clothes or a human with dog parts? This can lead to thoughts about the personification of pets who live very luxurious lives, or, perhaps, just a smile at the idea of a dog dressed up.

Bird Couple by Adnan Karabay, 17", polymer clay. Photo by Adnan Karabay

The Wallflower, Whennie, Asked to Dance by Connie Smith, 22", direct-sculpted porcelain, fabric, mixed media. Photo by W. Don Smith

■ Reasons for choosing to do animal figures are often varied. Connie Smith says that when she considered the doll-as-human-persona in commodity form, "it was an easy creative leap to other beings we think of as commodities, such as livestock, show animals, and pets." Wallflower Whennie's character originated from a train of thought stimulated by a World War II ration book, associations with USO dances, and the idea of unmarried women as commodities valued more for their inexperience. This led to contemplating the idea of simultaneous fear of and desire for experience. Whennie wants to know what it would be like to dance, but is at the same time afraid of what could happen. Could she fall in love? What would be required or happen to her self-ness if she did? As the artist developed the character, she essentially built a persona with sociological and psychological implications. Choices were made to complete the figure, such as type of animal, materials, and accessories. All were chosen to reflect the story. Connie relates that Whennie "even has a sculpted and embroidered body, jointed and padded to represent the secrets and capacities manifesting themselves in her clothed expression, fighting between 'flirt' or 'fight.' You might never see these elements, but they had to be there to complete the story for the artist.

Most of the innovative and imaginative artists engage in some sort of story line in their design development as well. The pieces that result are memorable because they make the viewer think about, and form an opinion about, what he is looking at...and if you ask the artist, he might tell you the story.

EXCEPTIONS, ARGUMENTS, AND EXCUSES

It's a given that not all people are identically shaped. For every typical body configuration, there can be any number of exceptions. On the other hand, people are more uniform than you think. You can't put the ears below the chin line or float them up to the top of the head, you can't make the jaw so narrow that a tongue and teeth can't be imagined inside, and you can't put knees in front of the calf muscle or the person couldn't walk. The same is true for figures. Unless your idea is extreme abstraction á la Picasso, even the most distorted figure you make has to look like it could function as a living being. Assuming correct joints and parts placement, even a big-headed cartoon character such as Charlie Brown can be seen as a functioning human. The charts you see here or in any art reference book are based on a common denominator of what the human body typically looks like. This is where you need to start when working on correct proportions and before you consider whatever variations you want to effect. Even those who do cartooning or who want to show an exceptional body shape are aware of the real, even though they might have the experience or ability to skip the steps between the real and the highly exaggerated.

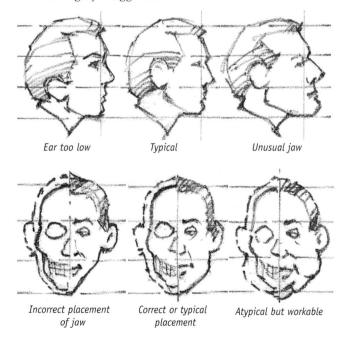

Ear too low   *Typical*   *Unusual jaw*

Incorrect placement of jaw   *Correct or typical placement*   *Atypical but workable*

The key to working well is consistency and the ability to defend, not justify, your choices. For instance, once I proudly showed a new sculpture to a colleague and she said, "Why did you make the elbow there?" The minute she said that, I realized I couldn't say why, and that clued me in to the fact that the elbow should not have been there. "Because I wanted it there" is not a good enough answer. "Because I did this, this, and this, so I had to do that" is a better answer.

DOLL OR TOY FORMS

Doll proportion is not the same as human proportion. Doll proportion is a function of the history of toymaking and its relation to public taste. When a figure maker is considering "making dolls" he needs to understand the difference between making dolls as in toy dolls and making dolls as in art figures. Dolls made in the toy tradition usually have big heads and small hands and feet. Bodies are fairly generalized and do not have a great deal of age-related detail. Costumes are made to be bright and pretty. Fit and realism are secondary to color and texture insofar as the manufacturer is willing to spend extra for better materials and construction. The contemporary toy fashion doll with her long legs, wasp waist, and generous bust (also small hands and feet) is so far out of human proportion it has become a joke. However, it does reflect the contemporary taste in toy dolls. This does not mean that all toy/play dolls are ugly or that people who like them have no taste. It means that there is an identifiable toy-doll type or genre and it is different. Know the difference. Avoid "doll-ness" when you don't want it, use it well when you do.

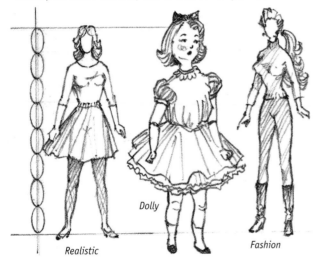

Realistic

Dolly

Fashion

TREATMENTS

The human, animal-like, or doll type of form can be executed within the bounds of realism, or it can be exaggerated/caricatured or abstracted.

Character and caricature have two different meanings in doll terms. Character in the antique collector's vocabulary actually means a very realistic or portrait type—a human personality as opposed to dolly type. Artists today often use the word character to define what is really a caricature or piece in which a few strong lines are used to delineate the essence of personality, often for humorous effect. Cartooning and caricature both depend on the abstraction and distortion of typical reality.

Abstraction accentuates or distorts a particular part or parts of a figure to emphasize form or line. If you are an artist who likes to do abstract, cartoon, or impressionistic figures, you might think this stuff about scale and proportion doesn't apply to you. Wrong. It does. And it is more difficult because you will have to invent your own well-designed proportional system. It is possible to have a poorly proportioned abstract or cartoon. Remember, everything you do has to have a pleasing and harmonious system—even if it is one you invent.

Here are some examples of exaggeration done well and not so well:

Well-done exaggeration

Realistic

Not-so-well-done exaggeration

ABSTRACTS AND IMPRESSIONS

The minute we say "abstract," many people immediately think "modern art." This isn't exactly the case. The first dimensional representations of the human figure were abstractions or impressions. The caveman saw his own form in a forked stick; he added bits of fur to it for clothing. Then he picked up a piece of charcoal and drew that stick figure on the wall of the cave. These figures were the result of his mind's ability to make the jump between the whole real object and the idea of the object. He didn't need to have a realistic representation, all he needed was a suggestion that could make him think "mighty hunter" or "harvest goddess." The same is true for the so-called "primitive" art of small children. Realism doesn't seem to have come into human representation until people wanted to record the likeness of a specific personality. A portrait in stone was a powerful reminder of the power of a king. The ancient Chinese emperor who had the likeness of every one of his soldiers done life-size in clay did it to emphasize two concepts: I have many men and they are many different individual men.

Choosing realism or impressionism is a function of need: How much detail do I need to provide to get the idea across? It is also a function of style: How much detail do you want to have? And, prior to the invention of the camera, choosing realism was a function of the need to make accurate recordings. Note that the development of contemporary impressionism parallels the development and popularity of the camera.

Nowhere in the world of figure making is the idea more important than in the execution of the human form in abstract or impressionistic style. It has also been said that those forms are the most difficult to do. Why? Because all of a sudden it seems there are no rules. There is no human model to copy from or to use as a critical guide.

Stop to think. In the history of dolls, how many really copy humans? Hardly any. Photographic realism in figure making is fairly rare and usually the province of portraiture and historical depictions. Play dolls have almost always been impressions of the human figure. Art figures reflect the artist's individual vision and his cultural background. Did a Victorian woman truly have the figure of the leather doll body of the era? No. How many children do you know that can be matched feature for feature to a toy doll of any era? What you see is an impression so successfully made you think it is realistic. You see a doll with a round face and large eyes and your brain identifies it as a child and fills in the gaps.

ABSTRACT

What does that mean? No holds barred? Anything goes? The idea of "anything goes" comes from a teaching mode that is used to encourage creativity in those who might be afraid of making something without a guide, a pattern, or at the very least a pictured goal. It works insofar as the human creator will almost invariably put some sort of organizing pattern into the work. This might be choosing a color scheme or cutting a pattern from a folded piece of paper.

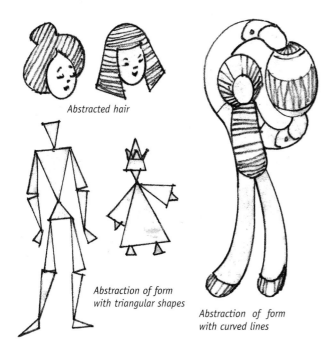

Abstracted hair

*Abstraction of form
with triangular shapes*

*Abstraction of form
with curved lines*

Oops! As soon as something like that is done, we introduce rules. We are right back to the beginning with the rules of design—in this case, balancing the form with the folded pattern, and rejecting colors that do not "go together."

In the doll world, the word abstract is often equated with chaotic. It takes a bit more work on the part of the viewer to recognize what is going on with an abstract piece. You could view an abstract as that something that has distilled some or several parts to their essence. For example, if you cut a piece of fabric and appliqué it onto a head, you have abstracted the idea of "hair-ness" to its most simple outline shape. If you reduce the human form to a set of triangles and circles, you have abstracted the shape.

As an artist, you could take one shape—the triangle—and emphasize it. You could then make a big triangular head with a small triangular body. You could put the sharper points of the triangle together or you could oppose them. As you can see, for the most part this is a thinking, organizing process.

Boneheads by Pamela Hastings, 18", fabric, bone, wood, wire, leather. Photo by Allen Bryan

MIND GAMES

Abstraction and impression—or for that matter, any figure or form—are the artist's creation of a small world unique unto itself. Any art form ought to be a mind game. It is a game for the artist to create the little world or piece of dimensional poetry. The finished creation should provide a few moments at least of gamesmanship for the viewer.

The viewer might not figure out what you think is there, but if you can provide him with a question to answer or a story to tell, or an emotion to feel when he looks at it, you are being successful as an artist. The concept of the figure as existing in its own world is a very valuable design tool as well. When you make decisions, make them based on what goes with the figure in its world, not your everyday world.

THE HASTINGS PIECES

■ Never make the mistake of thinking that because an artist does a piece that is "uncomfortable" it reflects on the artist's personality. The key thing is that the artist is able to see other phenomena, feel them, and interpret them for us. We don't have to know whether *Luna* reflects a bad day in the Hastings art studio or outside job, or if she was just empathizing with someone else's problems. In most cases, the artist is playing with an idea. When we look at *Luna*, we immediately get the impression of anger and frustration. Because of the multiple arms we can guess that the figure is angry or frustrated because it has too many things to do.

Depending on your persona, you could see this as either the figure or someone else imposing too long a list of things that need to be done. As an artist who spends a great deal of time sitting,

I do not feel legs are important. I know sit-down work can produce these emotions. Color symbolism is used either consciously or subconsciously and it reflects cultural associations. Red and purple are associated with anger. Black and gray are associated with depression. Other elements include the streakiness of the piecing, which looks like lightening. Here we feel an undercurrent of heavy-duty, powerful emotion. See the difference when the same idea of form is executed in softer color and textures. Do the titles make a difference to your interpretation? Should they?

ABOVE: *Luna* by Pamela Hastings, 18", cloth. Photo by Allen Bryan

BELOW: *Invocation Against Abuse* by Pamela Hastings, 18", cloth. Photo by Allen Bryan

CREATING AN ABSTRACTION

Can you make abstractions? If you can see faces in wallpaper or animals in clouds, then you probably can.

When I was working on the draft for this book, one of my colleagues said, "You ought to write something about how to make an abstract." When I got back to work on this section, I was toying with the "how-to" of it when I happened to look at my ironing board leaning up against the wall.

Here is the ironing board and its abstract form used for a figure.

I looked across the room and spotted a decorative bell. Here is the shape of the bell and here is the figure suggested from it.

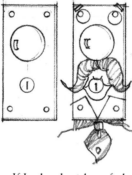

This can go on and on.

With these shapes I am personifying a non-human object. Another wonderful yet traditional form of abstraction in figure making is the emphasis of the shape of clothing. The human figure becomes the shape of its covering as in some of the traditional Japanese figures.

If I take the idea of clothing, and the idea that the clothing reflects the shape underneath, then I might do a lady like the one I sketched below. Notice how the form is composed of ovoid shapes. Even the hat is an oval. Here is a variation. This time the lady has a small hat, but the large idea is maintained by the boa around her neck.

The drawing suggests a two-piece fabric pillow shape. I could construct the body that way or I could design something a little more interesting by giving it a pear shape.

What for?

Most people think figures need to be realistic so they can understand them. Sometimes figures are just plain *fun* for the artist's amusement. Here is an idea I had that could be described as the personification of a pinwheel.

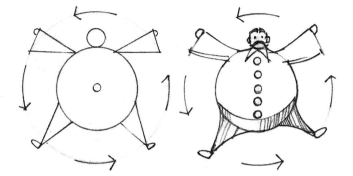

THE SURREAL

Literally, "above/over the real", surrealism appears to be a new trend in figure making. The best way to describe it is something like the disconnected elements of a dream state or hallucination. Where an impression might be a suggestion or fuzzy image, and an abstraction a broken or distorted image, the surreal is a construct of seemingly disconnected elements.

A RATIONALE

The minute I say with great authority that you should choose a well-defined type or form for your figure, someone will come up with a fairly reasonable exception. Furthermore, a good artist will pull off some unique version of form in a very successful piece. I will be standing there chewing on my hat brim! As a matter of fact, I can think of several artists who routinely combine doll form and abstraction, and throw in a helping of animal parts. However, the key is that the artist created his unique form in a way that shows thought and reasoning went into the process. All will have been for good effect. If he has done the job well, you won't be able to tell where one type begins and the other leaves off. Bottom line: If you like to be experimental, go ahead as long as it can be justified in your organizational system. If you like guidelines, stick to one particular type.

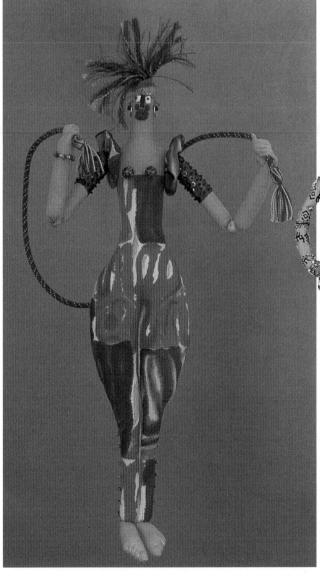

Neon by Deb Shattil, 22", cloth. Photo by Deb Shattil

Woman Spirit Talisman by Pamela Armas, vegetable-dyed, hand-blocked cottons, carved yak bone mask. Beaded loin-cloth by Harriet Turner. Photo by Charles Lundy

Jumping Jack by Deb Shattil, 12", cloth. Photo by Deb Shattil

Design Elements

The following are areas of design, or some of the areas of choice, that need to be considered, used, rejected, or reshaped as you organize your piece to give it maximum impact.

SUBJECT AND MOTIF

Part of the treatment of a form involves subordinate elements that help define it, the "underliners" so to speak. For instance, when we do a child and give it a toy to hold, the toy—a motif of childhood—helps define the figure and sharpen the impression it gives. If we do a Santa, we have a wide range of seasonal motifs that we can use to underscore "Santa-ness." If we do a bride, in western tradition, we have something old, something new, something borrowed, something blue to add. The older, more traditional bridal gifts of toaster and towels can be added. The motif can be a thing, or a texture, or a color association. The oft-interpreted poem "When I am an old woman" is usually identified by the purple costume, red hat, and walking stick.

FOCAL POINT

All dolls or figures are made in the round (and never forget the figure's backside needs to be as complete as the front). But every figure has a focal point—some particular area that the maker wants the viewer to focus in on in order to interact with it or understand its message.

If I ask you what the focal point of a piece is you will probably say "the head," and 90 percent of the time you will be right. That is where we look to ascertain the age and sex of the character and what emotional state the character is in.

The focal point could also be an interaction between the face and the hands. In particular the focus of the eyes on the hands...or the eyes focused on something in the figure's environment. It is very important to make sure that both eyes track on a held object or a second figure. When creating the design of your figure, you need to be sure you are going to direct the viewer's eye toward the part you want to emphasize.

You also need to double-check the focal point against your working point of view. For instance, if you work on a figure that stands twenty inches above your worktable and you work seated, you will be looking up at it as you work. You will, therefore, tend to work in the direction your eye sees the piece—upward. This means the figure will look fine to you—until you stand up. Then you should notice that you are seeing the figure in a very different perspective. As you work, take care to place the figure as you think it will be posed on a sale table, a gallery setting, or an owner's home. In general, it is good to plan your work so the viewer can easily see the face of the piece.

The Cat and the Cock by Elisabeth Flueler-Tomamichel, 21", LaDoll covered with paper, needlesculpted over wire armature. Photo by Elisabeth Flueler-Tomamichel

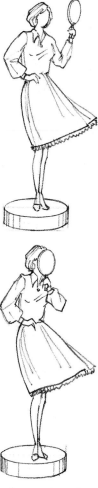

What if your piece is looking down? What if your piece is doing something in front of its face with its hands? If your piece is looking down you need to make sure that the top of the head and the part of the face that shows are well-executed from that angle. If your piece has something in front of its face—a hand holding a mirror—pose it so the viewer's sight line is slightly off center or so the face is in three-quarter or full profile. This, of course, means the profile will have to be interesting. Posing a figure means planning for how it will be seen. Sometimes a pose you like or want will have to be adjusted so the figure can be read to its best advantage.

LINE

Line plays a very important part in Retagene Hanslik's piece *Chad*. The first two things we note are strong vertical lines: the column and the figure leaning against it. Our feeling that a body in this position would need support against gravity is reinforced by noting that the column supports the body under the elbow. Then the line takes our eye from the column to the hand supporting the head. The paradox of this arrangement is that line has been used to make an artisitic statement (casual, relaxed) in the slanting of the body, but the actual body supporting lines (column and straight leg) remain strongly vertical. This

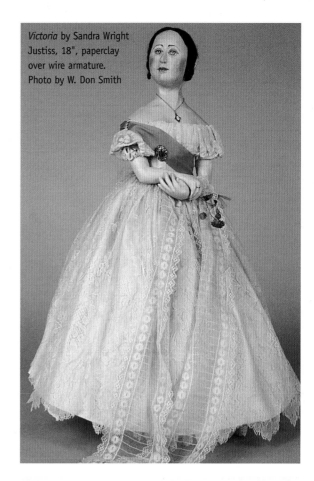

Victoria by Sandra Wright Justiss, 18", paperclay over wire armature. Photo by W. Don Smith

verticality is further enhanced by the straight arm. If we look more closely, we see there is also an underlying pattern of triangular lines in the crossed legs, the bent arm, and even in the jewelry. As a result, the figure is a vertically powerful piece that communicates a message of looseness. It is pleasing to us because of the thoughtful anomalous play of lines.

Occasionally a piece will be by its nature a stand-up, face-front type, as in a portrait of a famous queen. Here the message is straightforward, "This is how this person looked in her robes of state." The line of a piece like this might be emphasized by the positioning of the arms and the shape of the costume.

SCALE

Questions of scale are usually asked and answered by the phrases, "too big" or "too little". The print is too big for the doll's dress, or the shoes/feet are too little. Ask the question: Do all things relate to each other for the system I have chosen for this piece? If they don't match, is it a problem to fix or can I defend my choice?

Scale of the piece is determined by its height, and all of the parts should be done in relation to the overall size. A very easy mathematical job if your piece is going to be realistic, or a great challenge if you like to work with the unusual.

In either realistic or exaggerated figures, the world of the figure should determine the scale. All the materials, patterns, and objects in that world need to appear to belong to it.

Mathematically, it is easy to find scale by beginning with the size of the head. If the head is 2.5 inches from chin to top and you have decided it will be eight heads tall, the whole figure is 20 inches tall. If your figure was meant to represent a woman 5.5 feet tall in its world, then you divide the figure's height of 20 inches by the real-world height of 5.5, and you find that in the figure's world one foot is equal to 3.6 inches. Everything is just slightly less than one-fourth of your world. So, if I want this lady to hold a coffee mug that is 6 inches tall in my world, it has to be 1.8 inches in her world. If I want her to have one-inch ribbons in her hair, $^{1}/_{4}$-inch ribbon would be in scale with her world.

Chad by Retagene Hanslik, 18", Cernit. Photo by Alan Hanslik

Some ladies do carry very big purses, but few of them wear floral prints in which a single flower is as big as the width of the skirt. Some people have big feet, but practically none have feet three times the length of the hand. If you were to use a very large handbag with a figure in typical human proportions, you would need a good reason for doing so and you would have to be able to show how that reason worked with your design system. The viewer should not have any unanswerable questions.

I did a figure in typical human proportions except for one very large out-of-human-scale thumb. The viewer might question this momentarily, but just as quickly he should see that the thumb was spinning gold thread from wool. In just one small detail we introduce the element of fantasy, define a fairy-tale character, and underline the non-real result—gold thread—of the everyday act of spinning. The out-of-scale thumb becomes defensible. If you do what appears to be a pretty lady model figure who looks like she lives in the same world you do, and the viewer can't figure out why she has buttons as big as dinner plates and/or why she would wear them, then you have an element of scale that does not work in your overall system.

Panniere by Nancy Wiley, 22", figures are cast resin from original clay sculpture. Note how the artist has scaled the backdrop painting of the petticoat to fit the marionette figures who are played against it. Photo by Robert O'Brien

COLOR

Color in a figure, or the lack of it, is extremely important because of its psychological impact. It can also be used for subtle emphasis. Here are your most important considerations.

You can sculpt with color. Primary colors (red, blue, yellow), secondary colors (orange, purple, green), and intermediate colors (which combine one primary and one secondary color such as red-orange) can be mixed with white or black to form shades and tints. Lightness and darkness are important because by varying them within the hue, the artist can emphasize form or make elements stand out or recede. For instance, when painting a face, you can enhance the sculpted hollow cheek by painting it a darker shade or indicate light falling on higher places by lightening the hue.

Colors convey a feeling of temperature. Blue is termed cool and orange is termed hot by simple association with hot and cool things. The artist needs to select color temperatures that reflect the mood of his message.

The temperature of color suggests choices that need to be made about the body color or flesh tone of the figure. The more orange/yellow in skin tone, the better the figure will look in cool colors. The bluer in skin tone, the better it will look in warmer colors. Every material you can use in a body or face—clay, wood, polymer, or cloth—will have either a cool or warm tone. Furthermore, depending on batch and dye lot, even the same materials can vary.

Color also has scale. This is very tricky to describe. In essence it means that more pure

Party Animal by Sara Austin, 12", cloth.
Photo by Monty Jessop

hues, those closest to primary or secondary colors and intermediate mixes, will be too dominant on a small refined figure. It means that if you choose to do a small figure in pale blue, what you get off the bolt might be too intense or too bright. You might need a lighter, grayer blue to coordinate with the scale and proportion of the figure. Many artists routinely scale down fabric colors or make them less intense by tea-dying, gray shading with paint or dye, or by distressing the surface so it is not so highly reflective.

Color has a great deal to do with symbolism in a piece of art. The colors you use will provoke a certain response. Some colors have common associations. Pink makes a person think of valentines, freshness, babies, girls in Western culture. Western cultures associate white with brides, but Eastern cultures associate brides with red or cheerfulness, and white with mourning. Happy Santa in his red suit might be almost universally accepted as a cheerful fellow, but Father Christmas in a white robe might appear ghostly and spooky in some parts of the world. Always consider the emotional response possibilities when you choose color.

TEXTURE

Texture is the surface appearance or visual "feel" of the piece, and is very important to the costumed figure. Although the viewer might not usually touch the piece to appreciate it, his eyes translate the surface appearance to a sensual response. This part looks rough, or that part looks slick. Texture "speaks" so well that it is possible to deliver an entire message through texture and its variations without much color at all. Textures are every bit as psychologically loaded as colors. If you want the emphasis to be soft, cuddly, or sweet, you will pick plush, velvet, chiffon, or lacy textures. If you want to jar the viewer into an unexpected reaction, you might use a texture that is not normally associated with the concept. Again,

I Will Build A Ladder to the Sky
by Pamela Hastings, 16", cloth. Photo by Allen Bryan

any changes need to work within your system. When you put your baby figure in glossy vinyl, other elements must work together to convey your unique message about baby-ness.

PATTERN

Pattern is a repetition of any element that might appear in the figure. It is easiest for us to think of pattern as a fabric design repeat. We can also see pattern in a line of buttons or lines of decorative trim repeated on sleeves and around a skirt. Pattern can be thought of in a musical sense or as a series of dots and dashes. The pattern of the lines of trim might go wide, narrow, wide or wide-narrow.

Digger and the Garden Thieves by Marcie Hart, 18", Super Sculpey over wire armature. Photo by Ren Tromberg

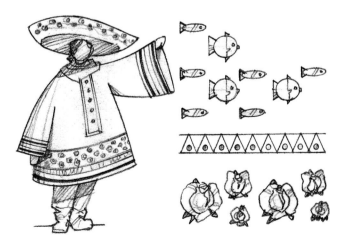

BALANCE

Balance has to do with weighting emphasis on elements of the figure. Symmetrical or even balance can be thought of as equal sides. One side has the same arrangement of parts as the other side—like a body with an arm on each side or a hairstyle with a center part and three curls on each side. Asymmetrical balance occurs when you have different things going on each side, but they equal the same weight or strength. This might happen when you put one large bow on the hip and two smaller bows on the opposite shoulder. *Checks and Balances* has two layers of meaning, and serves to illustrate the concept of asymmetrical balance in design to the extreme. The obvious message is that the clownish character is doing some sort of a balancing act with the rods. This message is reinforced by a number of elements and motifs throughout the piece. How many can you find? The face is divided into black and white, the rods in the hands are thick and thin and gold and silver. The costume is divided into checks and solids, and further underscored by having one wide sleeve and trouser leg and a narrower pair. The hanging trims are thicker on one side and thinner in texture on the other. As you can see, any or all of the elements we consider in design can play a part in balance.

HARMONY

Harmony, in my definition, is when the above-mentioned elements are so well-incorporated in a design that no single element stands out or interferes with the meaning or message. It is the balanced relationship of all the visual stimuli—proportion, scale, line, texture, and color.

It does not take much of a leap to realize that the elements of design essentially create the psychology of the doll. We assume the maker wants to make an impression, that he wants the viewer to appreciate his piece. How does he do that? By putting together things that will spark identification with the viewer's emotions about people or dolls. The figure goes out in public to be seen and judged against social and psychological views. Just like a person, at the extremes it can stand out for its differences and eccentricities or it can blend. It can make someone say "aah, yes" or it can make someone say "Oops, what's going on?" And, just like a person, it should be known for its individuality, its specific combination of character traits that make it different from the next one.

Checks and Balances by Susanna Oroyan, 20", Sculpey. Photo by W. Don Smith

STYLE

Anyone who makes figures is an individual, and the way he assembles the various elements of a figure—the character, size, colors, textures, shapes, and types—will form a distinctive, personal style. Individual style evolves, and is recognizable after a number of pieces have been done. And, just to make it more interesting, an artist might change his style or have several styles. For instance, I have three styles of expression in cloth dolls, one involving a rather faceless form. Another involves use of texture and pattern with white-on-white, another involves painting on the form and figure. I can do needlesculpture, I can do molded faces, but most of my ideas will involve shape and pattern, or surface design in cloth with the resulting figures falling into the abstract type. elinor peace bailey is a colorist with a background in quilting. Ideas will come to her in a style that involves putting together pieces of very colorful fabrics.

elinor peace bailey used the concept of individual style and one's discovery of it in her book, *Mother Plays with Dolls*. She designed a basic pattern shape, what she calls a "modular doll," and sent it to twenty artist friends. Every single one of the twenty dolls that resulted reflected the individual maker's own style. Without looking for names, I could identify Jean Ray Laury's distinctive use of felt, Sally Lampi's eyes, Barbara Chapman's beaded embellishment, and I wasn't surprised to see Marinda Stewart's ruffles and lace, Mary Mashuta's quilted vest, or Lisa Lichtenfel's very realistic eye. Mine, of course, had the only sculpted face. Body parts had been elongated, embroidered, taken apart and jointed or turned to give dimension, painted, dyed, and needle sculpted. Each artist had applied his or her inclinations, technical knowledge and imagination to create something that was undoubtedly their own and at the same time a new version of the concept of doll-ness or a new perspective on the human condition. Furthermore, each one had enjoyed the challenge of the problem solving and the excitement of discovering the best solution...and that's what doll design is all about.

Lido by Van Craig, 32", paperclay, textiles, fur.
Photo by Malcolm J. Magri

Garla or Gargoyle Girl by Lisa Lichtenfels, 20", mixed media with nylon skin.
Photo by Lisa Lichtenfels

The Whole Body

Play toys, comic exaggerations, beautiful fashion ladies, or cats in hats—most of the figures we make are going to say something about the human condition. Most are going to have the human body as a reference point or, most likely, the main point. There are a few design considerations to keep in mind when working with the human form.

HEADS

Figure makers tend to be guided by the idea of personality as depicted in the head of the piece. This is quite natural as we tend to identify and react to people by their facial expressions. The maker often gets his ideas by doodling with cloth or clay until a head with a personality appears. If we concentrate on finishing the head, it can be a big pitfall on the path to a well-designed figure. We either base the rest of the design and construction on the head, or we overdo the head and let the rest just sort of happen below it.

There are a few things you can do to avoid a "head dominant" piece. First, try not to begin with a preconceived picture. Let your initial concept stay loose while you play with the material. (You can do this even if you are working with a specific personality in mind.) Make several sketches in the clay or cloth or on paper. Usually each one will have a special aspect that can be developed. Next, for each rough head, the minute its personality asserts itself, immediately start to visualize or sketch the rest of the body and its pose. Example: This head reminds me of a little old man. What is he doing? He is sitting hunched forward over his cane. Or, he is a shaman in a meditation trance. Or, give him elf-like ears and he is peeking out from behind a tree stump. Each one of these visualizations will require a whole different approach to the body and the way it works with the head.

If you can explore the numerous possibilities, you won't end up trying to force one notion when it might not be the best solution.

When you choose a pose before the head is fully finished, you can be sure the necessary angle of the head and neck and the focal track of the eyes are reflected in your full figure. For example: a figure with its head turned to the side looking at something in its hand will require not only tilting the head, but sculpting a shortened neck tendon on one side, lengthened on the other, and shaping the eye process to reflect correct flesh and muscle.

When you have an idea of pose, keep in mind costume styles, actual materials, and technical processes for assembly. Make sketches of these or write yourself some notes.

When you do this, you will find that some notions won't work with others or that some ideas will require you to consider specific types of construction in order to make the figure. Don't worry about having a lot of extra, unfinished heads. A big part of the artist's job is experimental and educational play. You'll toss the bad ideas and finish the good ones.

If sketching is not your natural "thing," there are a few ways to rough out a pose without a pencil. You can build your sketch as a clay or wax model. You can use a jointed, posable wooden artist model or build a template. You can build a working wire armature. Or, you can use yourself or another human. When I was developing the *Dollmaker* figures (pages 6, 7), I spent considerable time in front of a mirror looking at myself in several poses. When I did the third piece, *Heads to Finish* (page 10), I became more interested in the mechanics of the frame of heads. I neglected to consider the whole body anatomy and, naturally, ended up with a big problem to fix before I was finished. However you go about it, coordination of all the body parts from the beginning is the prime factor in making the best figure.

GESTURE OR POSE?

Many artists use the word *gesture* to refer to characterization given by body posture. This comes from the figure drawing class where quick sketches of a pose are made. When I think of the word gesture it is in regard to movement. He made an obscene gesture. She made a gesture of resignation. For me, this means an outward signal of an inward condition—an isolatable movement like a shrug or the position of a hand. If pushed, however, I think the artists who use the word gesture would probably accept the word *posture*. Body language is perhaps an even better term. It is the whole posture of the character that must reflect the emotional content of the character you wish to portray. The person who shows resignation will not only have slumped shoulders, he will have slightly bent knees, his feet will look flat and planted, his head will be down, his eyes might be slightly closed, the facial musculature will be lax. The person who makes the rude gesture will probably have his shoulders back and his chin and chest thrust out. In both cases the body language will back up that one signal. It has to for the figure to express the idea.

Ace of Acorns by Kathryn Walmsley, 12", Cernit and paperclay, cloth over wire armature body. Photo by Paul Schult

Body posture and gait will change form. Consider: A man hurrying through a crowded city street will pull his arms close to his body and thrust his head and shoulders forward. A man covering ground in open space will let his arms swing, pull his body up, and take long, loping steps. A hunter in the jungle will walk on the balls of his feet in a tip-toe fashion. Always remember that the body is jointed.

In a crowd   In open space   Hunting or stalking

When bones move to hold a particular pose, the form of the body will be changed. For instance, when a figure is standing on one foot and stepping out with the other, the hip will be higher on the stationary leg. Any good anatomy book or drawing text will show interior bone structure as it relates to various movements. Always check to be sure the external form reflects the right bone placement for the pose you are showing. If your sculpture is going to be refined and realistic, you will have to consider the expansion and contraction of muscles and tendons in various poses as well. Most of the major problems in achieving a successful figure relate to its form more than its assembly.

ILLUSIONS AND DELUSIONS

What people know is correct and what they want to see can be two different things. We tend to think of a beautiful woman as being proportioned with long legs. This is a cultural phenomenon, not the norm. The human body is actually divided pretty equally at the pelvic line, which makes the legs look short. Compared to the female, a man has wider shoulders and smaller pelvis. The paperback novel cover shows these male characteristics, but most normal males would have to do quite a bit of weightlifting to get that shape. Our children are not darlings of anatomical perfection, either. A child of eight might have huge ears, big teeth, not much of a nose, large hands, and small feet, all reflecting parts growing at different rates. The ideal, however, is an important part of our consideration of the human condition, and we all appreciate seeing it in a figure. Remember, when you choose to represent the ideal, it reflects a cultural preference and not what the artist's anatomy books will show you or what you might sketch in a life drawing class. Here again, you will need to create the system that says ideal to your viewer.

Hero   Ordinary   Toothy kid

PROPORTION

Sometimes you will hear a comment like, "the body is out of proportion." What is proportion? Put simply, proportion is the pleasing arrangement of parts. For artistic purposes, it is a pleasing (i.e. acceptable) arrangement that clearly communicates the maker's idea. The arrangement is the idea, and at the same time underlines or emphasizes the idea. Proportion, like design, has basic elements common to all cultures. These elements, which we think of as harmonious arrangements, come from nature—the arrangement of leaves on a twig or the fractals of a crystal—and can be mathematically described. Leaves on a stem may be arranged exactly opposite one another (1:1), or the chambers of a shell may be arranged in an ascending order of size (1, 1.5, 2, 2.5, etc.). You can invent the system, and determine the proportional scheme. And for those of you who say "Yes, but..." remember that it is possible to write a mathematical formula for the seemingly erratic motion of a single falling leaf. If we did not have a sense of common natural proportion we would have no need to have terms like "disfigured" and "disproportionate."

If it is "out of proportion" it will not be true to a typical human form; a fashion figure has legs that are disproportionately long compared to the typical female. Alternately, it will have an element that doesn't work in your system—perhaps your mermaid's tail is three times as long as the torso when it shouldn't be any longer than legs. If your purpose is to show a beautiful lady with a fish tail, then a longer tail will draw the viewer away from the torso and face. Make a longer tail *only* *if* you can make the viewer understand a reason for it.

Here we go. Let's see if we can find some methods and shortcuts for your technical reference. Warning: Be aware that there is danger in being overly correct. It can be mechanical and boring. These are meant to be aids to acceptable forms. Use systematic variations when you want to create a different type.

BASIC HUMAN PROPORTIONS

The drawings on the following pages show the adult figure based on a system of eight heads being equal to total height. This makes a slightly taller figure with a lit-tle compensation for foreshortening. Average human pro-portions for one-, three-, and nine-year-old children are also shown. Keep in mind that children often grow at dif-ferent rates, and adult types may be tall and thin or short and stocky.

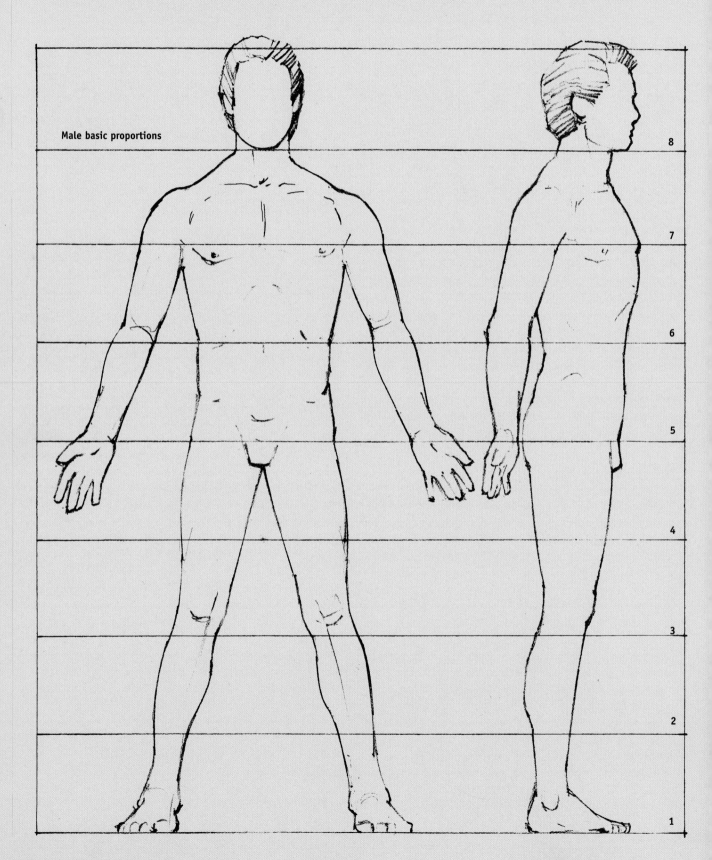

Male basic proportions

8

7

6

5

4

3

2

1

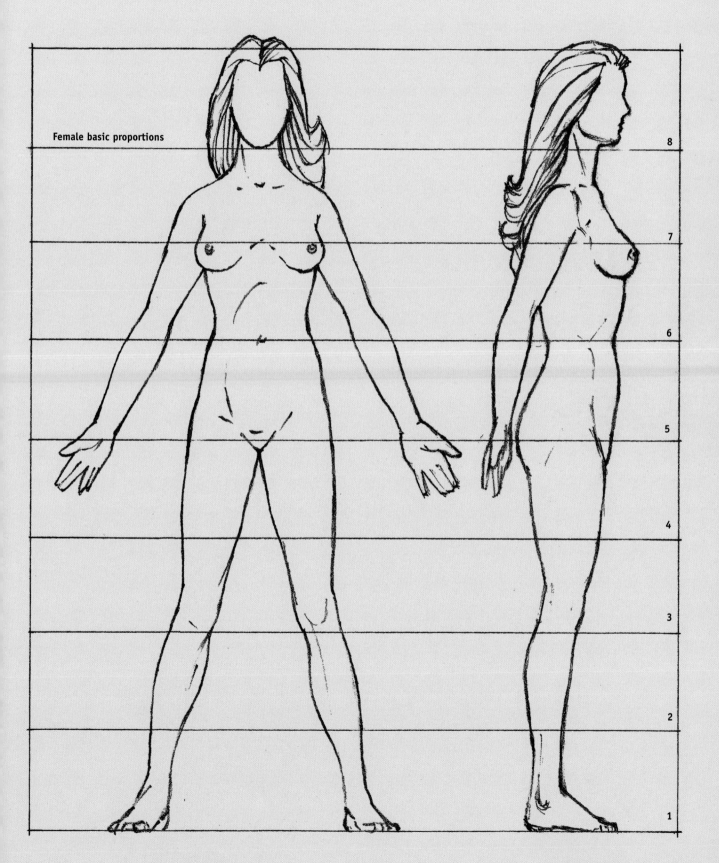

Female basic proportions

8

7

6

5

4

3

2

1

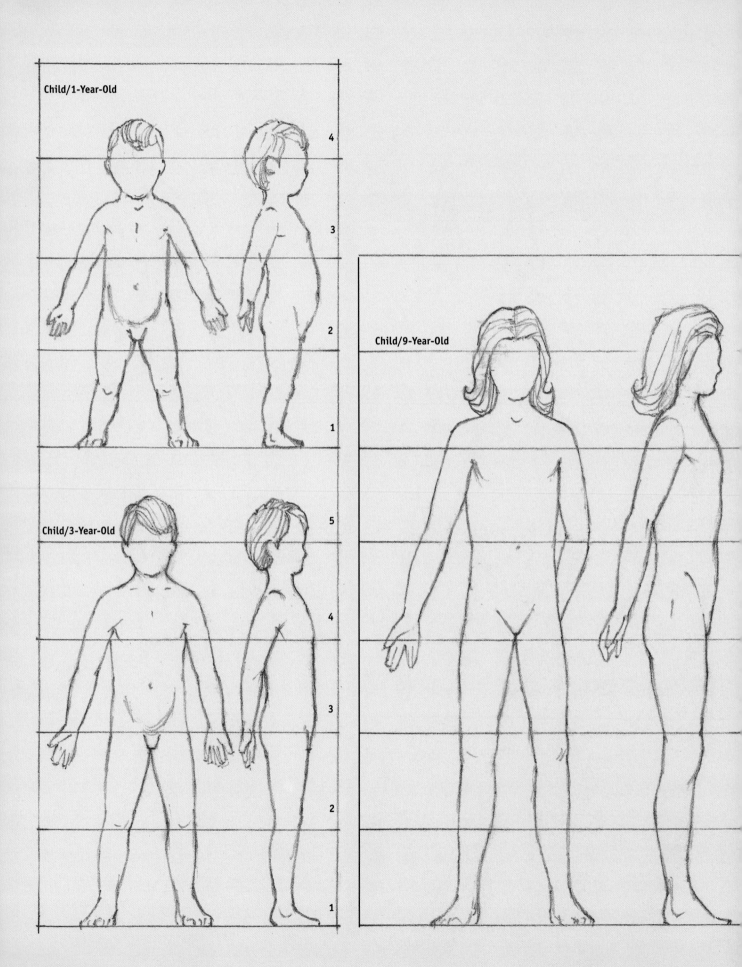

Child/1-Year-Old

4

3

2

1

Child/9-Year-Old

Child/3-Year-Old

5

4

3

2

1

DESIGNING WITH BASIC BODY DRAWINGS

ENLARGING AND REDUCING

Trace the basic adult female shown on page 47. Cut the drawing apart at calf and mid-thigh and pull the pieces apart. Measure the head height of the basic drawing. If you want your fashion lady very tall (nine heads), add one half-head measurement to the thigh and one half-head to the calf. If you want a moderately tall figure, add one-fourth to each space. Redraw the lines.

If you want to make the body drawing fit a head you are sculpting, measure that head from the chin to the top of the head. Multiply the measurement by the total desired body height in heads and enlarge your drawing on a photocopier until it measures that height.

Example: The head is 2.5 inches tall. Multiply 2.5 times 8.5 or 9 to get finished height.

To enlarge a male figure in the same way, cut your drawing and increase space equally (one-third of a head for a 9-heads-tall figure) at waist, thigh, and calf. Any time you add length to the body from neck to hip, be sure to add length to the arms as well. Note that a female fashion figure is usually more slender than the typical female. Adjust your drawing accordingly. This same method of lengthening (and shortening) can be used to create a body shape for fantasy figures such as elves and fairies...assuming you think little people look pretty much like humans!

You don't have to be a graphic artist to do this. All it takes is the ability to cut apart, trace, redraw, and use a photocopier.

DEVELOPING PATTERNS

Trace the body form you want. Enlarge it to the finished height you want the body to be. Adjust the drawing to fit the character or body type that you need. For instance, if you want a fat person, enlarge the width of the pattern. Make a photocopy and cut it apart at the joint areas or at the shoulders if you want separate arms that will hang naturally at the sides. Note that a flat, two-sided stuffed cloth body will always "take up" when stuffed. The resulting body will be thinner than your drawings. Refer to the section on Cloth Figures for ways to add dimension to your pattern. Always be prepared to do several experimental forms in order to achieve a good final result.

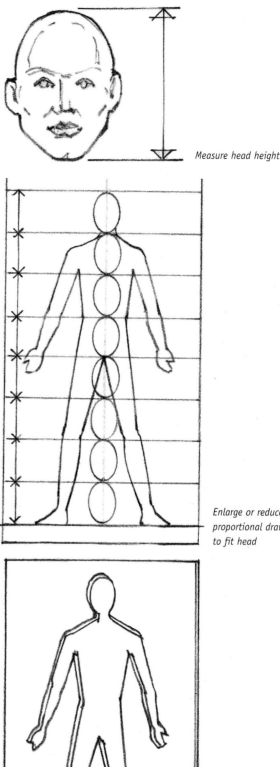

Measure head height

Enlarge or reduce proportional drawing to fit head

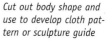

Cut out body shape and use to develop cloth pattern or sculpture guide

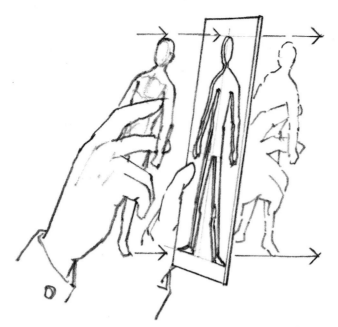

Use template to check sculpture. The widest part of the head should fit the cut-out paper as closely as possible.

MAKING A TEMPLATE

When you have adjusted the basic form or your original drawing to the size and height desired, a template can be made for checking sculpture. Trace your drawing on a sheet of heavy paper (like cardstock or thin cardboard) and cut out the form as you would for a stencil. Handling templates as you work is easier if you cut separate ones for the head, arms, legs, and torso. Make templates for both side and front views. As you work, add sculpture material until the figure or part of the figure being worked on fits the space. Artist Robert McKinley used these cut-out parts to create interior cardboard armatures for many of his sculptures. This process is discussed in detail in his book *Dollmaking: One Artist's Approach.*

If your figure is to be a portrait of a particular person, it would be helpful and more accurate to photograph your subject in a bathing suit in full front view and full side view. Templates and patterns can be made by enlarging the photographs to the desired height for the figure.

If you tend to start by sculpting a head, you can do that first. Lay the head out and create a set of templates scaled to its size. For typical realistic scale, the adult body will be 7.5 times the length (top to chin) of the head. Figures, however, are often viewed from above. This has a foreshortening effect; a correctly proportioned figure might appear to be short and stumpy. In order to compensate for this some artists make their adult figures 8 heads high, or in the case of a fashion figure, 8.5 heads high. The following table provides shortcuts to calculate the height of a finished piece using realistic anatomical proportions.

PROPORTION CHART

Head height	Head height x 7.5 = body height	Head height x 8 = body total	Head height x 8.5 = body total
1.0	7.5	8	8.5
1.25	9.4	10	10.6
1.5	11.25	12	12.75
1.75	13.1	14	14.9
2.0	15.0	16	17.0
2.25	16.9	18	19.1
2.5	18.75	20	21.25
2.75	20.6	22	23.4
3	22.5	24	25.5

Doll house / miniature scale 1 inch = 1 foot

- To begin developing the body proportion for your head, pick the proportional drawings to fit the correct age for your character. Enlarge a proportional drawing until you have three or four copies with heads the same size or near to the size of your head. Cut out the head on your paper copy. Insert your sculpted head. Does it fit? If necessary, repeat, cutting out your other copies to find a paper template your head will exactly fit into. Fit the head *into* the paper template because when just laid on top, there can be some small but important optical illusions that will start you off in the wrong direction. Templates are always used to fit *around* the sculpted form.

- When you have found the proper fit for your head, the remainder of the proportional drawing you use will be in correct proportion to your head. Now you can begin to work on posture or pose by cutting apart the rest of the drawing. Play with the parts to find a pleasing pose that accentuates the idea of the character you wish to communicate.

- Lay tracing paper over your selected arrangement and make a character sketch of your figure. Be sure to make the appropriate adjustments for bone and muscle placement. For instance, if your figure is going to stand on tiptoe or wear high-heeled shoes, the bones in the foot will arch and the muscles of the calf will bunch a bit more.

- Use your character drawing to make a template from cardstock or thin cardboard for each body part to be sculpted.

- Continue to construct your figure, occasionally checking your shapes by inserting the parts into the paper templates you have made.

- Label your sketches and templates and save them for future dolls with similar sized heads and for costume pattern drafting.

UPPER LEFT: *Mack Kandinsky* by Chris Chomick and Peter Meder, 21", wood armature, loose hinge joints with soft, pellet-filled body. Photo by Chris Chomick

LOWER LEFT: *My Mentor Ronnie* by Angela Talbot, 14", Sculpey. Photo by Trudie Lee

UPPER RIGHT: *Daddy's Little Darling* by Jolene Thompson, 18", Super Sculpey, cloth over wire armature. Photo by W. Don Smith

Nonesuch by Bill Nelson and Tom Banwell, 18", resin and mixed media. Photo by Dennis McWaters

LOWER LEFT: *Lunar Eclipse* by Sandra Thomas Oglesby, 16", paperclay. Photo by Sandra Thomas Oglesby

UPPER LEFT: *Marley's Ghost* by Nancy J. Laverick, 17", cloth.
Photo by Nancy J. Laverick

UPPER RIGHT: *Junior Birdman* by Carroll Stanley, 20", Cernit.
Photo by Carroll Stanley

LOWER RIGHT: *Snow Monkeys* by Adnan Karabay, 16",
polyform over wood, hand-detailed sleigh created by artist.
Photo by Adnan Karabay

UPPER LEFT: *Ransom* by Judith Klawitter, 24", Super Sculpey, wire armature. Photo by Mark Bryant

UPPER RIGHT: *Delivery* by Sandra Thomas Oglesby, 11", Super Sculpey/ Promatt, cloth over wire armature. Photo by Sandra Thomas Oglesby

LOWER RIGHT: *Veronica* by Joanne Gelin, 12" seated, one-of-a-kind stone clay on soft body with movable arms. Photo by Joanne Gelin

UPPER LEFT: *Renaissance Woman* by Carol A. Stygles, 16", head of polymer clay with photocopied transfer on silk face. Photo by Rod Soat

LOWER LEFT: *Pandora* by Robin Foley, 10"x 26", sculpted cloth. Photo by Fly-by-Night Graphics

UPPER RIGHT: *Daydreams* by Karen Cadiou, 12", Cernit over wire armature. Photo by Karen Cadiou

UPPER LEFT: *The Squashbuckler* by Pattie Bibb, 16", paperclay over cloth. Photo by W. Don Smith

UPPER RIGHT: *Rose Nose Fertility God* by Sara Austin, 20", socks, fabric, buttons. Photo by Monty Jessop

LOWER RIGHT: *Songhai* by Lawan Angelique, 10" x 12" seated, cloth sculpture. Photo by Chris Florkowski

LOWER LEFT: *Arthur* by Martha Boers and Marianne Reitsma, 15", Super Sculpey on wire armature, cloth body. Photo by Marianne Reitsma

UPPER RIGHT: *Madame Blue* by Marie-Claude Dupont, 20", Super Sculpey over wire armature. Photo by Martin Delisle

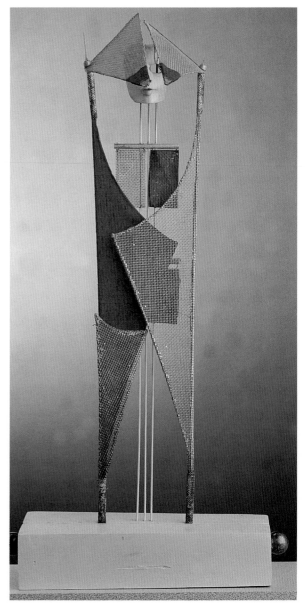

UPPER LEFT: *Japonica* by Akiko Anzai, 14", cloth with cloth over paperclay face. Photo by Akiko Anzai

RIGHT: *No Face Left To Lift* by Hennie Koffrie, 24", woven metal, paper, silk, and paperclay. Photo by Laurens Janus

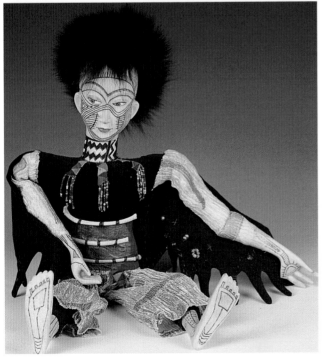

UPPER LEFT: *Renaissance Doll* by Uta Brauser, 21", porcelain. Photo by John Martini

LOWER LEFT: *Magic Man* by Caty Carlin, 17", carved and jointed wood. Photo by Caty Carlin

UPPER RIGHT: *Renaissance Angel* by Janet Ouren, 25", Super Sculpey and Cernit. Photo by W. Don Smith

TOP: *Baroque Musicians* by Barbara Chapman, wire armature, paperclay. Photo by Bob Hirsch

LOWER LEFT: *Doll-in-a-Box* by Lawan Angelique, 16", paperclay, wire armature, painted, hinged box. Photo by Chris Florkowski

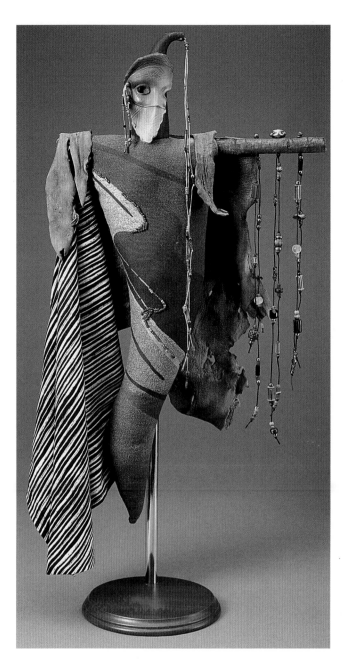

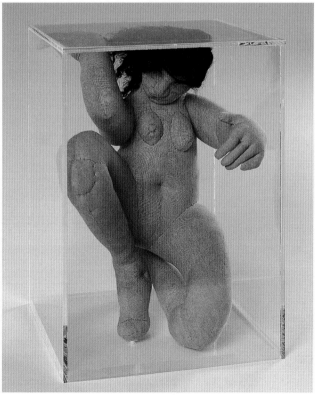

UPPER LEFT: *Male Shaman* by Gabriel Cyr and Sandy Blaylock, 24",
fiber, leather, gourd, copper, beads, and shell. Photo by Martin Fox

UPPER RIGHT: *Memories* by Nancy Walters, 15" seated, porcelain,
direct sculpture. Photo by Nancy Walters

LOWER RIGHT: *Turning 50* by Beverly Dodge Radefeld, 12",
cloth in fiberglass case. Photo by David Matthews

As a dollmaker creates small-scale representations of people, he must learn to reproduce all the things that people might have, use, or wear in the real—and in the imagined—world. There are no special tools or materials just for dollmaking. The artist adapts materials from the real world to suit his needs.

Most things that an artist needs can be found at craft, fabric, art, and hardware stores. Some of these things, like laundry starch, garden string, and white glue, are surprisingly ordinary. Each artist will find certain tools fit his hand better. As in design and construction, you have to experiment with a

variety of materials to discover those that work well for you. Over the years, an artist will accumulate an enormous stock of interesting and inspirational "stuff." It makes him happy to know it's there, even if he never has a reason to use it (or be able to find it). He will also learn or teach himself a number of craft skills, ranging from metalwork and mold making to photography, word processing, and accounting. He will also "collect" more paraphernalia to do it with. Along the side of the page are a few things most of us would agree form the basic things a figure maker should have on hand.

computer
phone/fax
sewing machine
water-based clay
plasticine clay
air-drying clay
polymer clays
good lights
wire
plaster
plaster bowl and spatula
mold forms
rubber mold material
eyes
hair stuff
mirror
sculpture tools
sculpture table
coffee
sculpture-working armature
drills, hammers, saws, vices, and pliers
chisels, files
hardware: rings, washers, nails
a view out the window
camera
photo background and lighting
books
magazines
cat/dog
TV/radio
bulletin board
sketchbook
paints, pens, pencils
scissors
sewing basket stuff
buttons
snack food
laces, trims, ribbons
fabric
fabric
fabric
stuffing, batting
string
comfortable chair
wax
beads
threads and yarns
iron, ironing board, pressing hams
pleater

Molds

Mold making? Here? Now? Yes, absolutely. Every kind of figure maker should know how to make and use molds. Usually, we think of a mold as a plaster form necessary for casting originals in liquid materials such as porcelain. Usually, an artist considers using a mold because he wants to make multiples of a finished figure, such as a limited edition, in porcelain. However, editions can be cast in liquid paperclay and the increasingly popular resins. Polymer clays can be pushed/pulled from molds as well, and many fabric dollmakers are using them to make masks or limbs that are covered with fabric or painted. Equally important, molds can be used as an aid to the thinking and engineering of a figure; you will see this process in the example of Erin Libby's development of the *PinPon* character (page 70).

A thorough discussion of molds and mold making would require book-length treatment in itself. Here, we want to introduce the general concepts and considerations so the possibility exists in your design repertoire. Products and reference materials are listed under Suppliers (pager 156). Don't hesitate to talk to materials suppliers as they will take the time to work with you to find the best materials and methods to achieve your goals.

Quick Reference

- *Original model or pattern=the sculpture that will be used to make a mold*

- *Casting=the copy that comes out of the mold. Castings may be formed by pouring liquid materials into the mold or pushing in and pulling out soft, moist materials.*

- *Mold=negative shape of plaster, or flexible material formed over the original*

- *Jacket=plaster formed over a mold made of flexible material. The jacket keeps the mold from warping. The jacket is sometimes called a "mother mold."*

TO MOLD OR NOT TO MOLD

Before deciding whether to use a mold, you need to consider your original sculpture material. If it is a water-soluble material such as paperclay, or a sculpture with undercuts (dips in the surface that will hook and hold the mold material and keep it from releasing the original), you will need to make a flexible mold. These are referred to in the generic sense as rubber molds. Flexible molds can be made with latex that is painted on over the original, or with elasticon or RTV (a type of rubber) that is poured into a cavity. There is also a flexible wax that some artists use for impression molds.

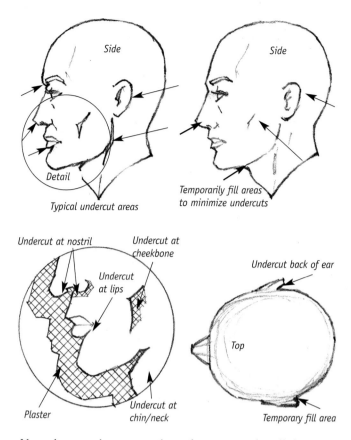

Side

Side

Detail

Typical undercut areas

Temporarily fill areas to minimize undercuts

Undercut at nostril

Undercut at cheekbone

Undercut at lips

Undercut back of ear

Top

Plaster

Undercut at chin/neck

Temporary fill area

You also need to consider what material will be cast (poured) or pulled from the mold to make your final product. If you will be making a mold that you push the material into and pull it out of, you will probably need a very slick-surfaced mold with little or no porosity. Paperclay, polymer clay, wax, and resin require this kind of mold. If your material is liquid ceramic slip, water-based clay, or one of certain types of composition, you will need a mold that will draw water. This kind of a mold is made of plaster. If your sculpture is undercut, castings will not release from a hard plaster mold.

A CLEAN ORIGINAL: THE WAX MODEL

Most sculpting figure makers prefer to sculpt the first or original form in plasticine or polymer clay. A flexible "rubber" mold or a plaster mold requires a very smooth and uniform surface to create a good casting. Cleaning off bumps or irregularities in a porcelain casting is time-consuming, and in a resin casting can often cause more surface problems. For these reasons, many artists make molds of their original clay work, cast a wax model from the mold, and then clean up or tool the wax until it is glassy smooth and ready to be used to make a final mold from which the finished forms will be cast. Wax castings or tooling models are especially useful for experimenting with jointing cuts and movement and for exploring variations of the character. You can see and be sure the joint will work, or you can play with facial expressions until you find the best combination.

THE PLASTER MOLD

A good, professional quality, multiple-part block-and-case mold is required for casting ceramic slip or porcelain. Essentially, the plaster draws moisture from the poured liquid slip until the slip becomes firm enough to remove from the mold. Plaster molds can be used for casting wax only if they are soaked in soapy water and dried or otherwise coated with a material that will prevent wax from sticking to the plaster. Since the pores of the plaster are filled in (by wax or coatings), plaster molds used for casting wax cannot be used for pouring porcelain. In making a plaster mold it is vital to eliminate all undercut areas or to place parting lines so the mold parts can be pulled away without damage to the casting.

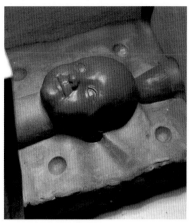

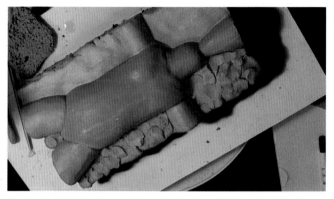

Heather Maciak begins her mold by setting her clay original on a bed of soft plasticine clay. The funnel shape of brown clay at the top will become a hollow channel for pouring the porcelain slip into the mold. Note the clay plugs at shoulders and hips. These will allow a solid, hollow casting to be made. After the casting is made, openings for jointing materials to pass through will be cut away.

Head in its clay bed surrounded by the mold box form. Note that as the part line will run around the edge of the ear, a corresponding hollow has been made in the clay bed. In the next step, the fourth side of the mold form will be clamped on, and the resulting box will be filled with plaster to make one half of the mold. When the plaster has set, the mold box will be turned over and the clay bed removed. The poured plaster mold, covered with a releasing agent, now becomes the bed for the pouring of the second half of the mold. Notice that the area of the plaster mold around the original parts is approximately twice the width of the parts. This is to allow the plaster to completely draw the moisture from the poured porcelain.

Both parts of the mold for casting legs. Marbles are pressed into the clay mold bed so depressions are formed that will key the mold parts together for a smooth fit.
The photo on the left shows the original clay legs set on clay bed. Notice that the upper leg has been sculpted to fit into openings at the torso hip area for jointing, and the pour holes are placed so extra poured material may be cleaned off neatly.

Angelica by Heather Maciak, 13",
porcelain. Left photo by Heather
Maciak, right photo by W. Don Smith

THE ELASTICON MOLD

Much of the technical information used by master figure makers comes from other trades and crafts outside the doll world. With regard to molds, I learned as much or more by engaging my dentist in mold discussions while trying to keep my mind off nasty procedures going on in my mouth. It occurred to me that the stuff he was using to make molds of my teeth that hardened in only a few minutes would be just the thing for making quick molds in my studio. The material we decided would work best for me is called Syringe Elasticon®. There is one catch: it is relatively expensive and is available only from dental supply houses. One small doll, or perhaps two to four heads, can be cast from a kit. However, I find it quite satisfactory. In most cases I use it for making molds of faces or just the front half of the doll head. It is rare for me to make more than four or five molds a year with it. Other silicon mold products come in larger quantities and have a limited shelf-life, so this product works well for me. Usually, other non-undercut parts of a piece can be cast with a plain plaster mold. Surprisingly, when given a plaster jacket, these quickie molds hold up for over fifty castings or pressings.

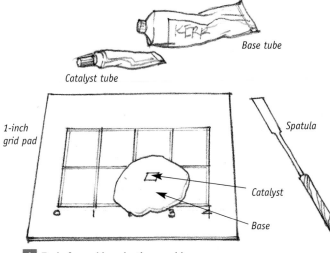

A Tools for making elasticon molds

Base tube

Catalyst tube

1-inch grid pad

Spatula

Catalyst

Base

Here is how I make a simple mold using the dental elasticon material:

1. I use the grid sheet that comes in the kit when I am ready to mix the elasticon base with its catalyst as shown in Figure A.

2. My original sculpted head (of any hard material) is pushed into a block of soft Styrofoam so the back of the head to the ear is buried. The plasticine modeling clay is pressed around the head and flattened to form a ¼-inch-thick collar or flange extending about two inches from the head. You can see this base and collar in Figure B. A very light coating of liquid soap can be applied to reduce formation of air bubbles.

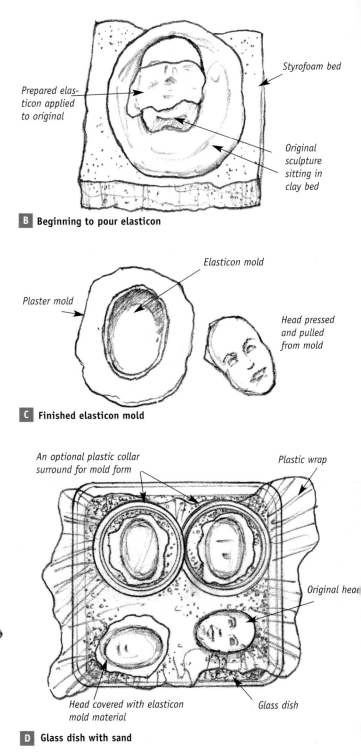

Prepared elasticon applied to original

Styrofoam bed

Original sculpture sitting in clay bed

B Beginning to pour elasticon

Elasticon mold

Plaster mold

Head pressed and pulled from mold

C Finished elasticon mold

An optional plastic collar surround for mold form

Plastic wrap

Original head

Head covered with elasticon mold material

Glass dish

D Glass dish with sand

3. When the bases and catalyst are mixed uniformly, I use the spatula to pour the mixture over the exposed head as shown in Figure B. I begin by pouring the mixture over the eye and nose area. Four or five mixtures may be needed to cover the exposed head. The material is viscous enough so it will not usually run more than a half inch onto the clay collar beyond the head. The mixture will begin to firm up very quickly, and the elasticon material will be ready to cover with plaster within an hour.

4. When the elasticon is set (not sticky to the touch), I mix plaster and let it set to the consistency of whipped cream. I then spoon the plaster over the elasticon mold in its Styrofoam base. This makes what is called a "clamshell" or free-form mold jacket. When the plaster has set, the original head and elasticon mold is removed from it. The elasticon is lifted away from the head and returned to the plaster mold jacket. Figure C (page 66) shows the plaster jacket containing the elasticon mold after the head has been removed. The mold is now ready to be used.

5. I can press paperclay or polymer clay into this mold to get an impression casting of the front half of the head. A very light dusting of talcum powder in the mold will help release the molded material. Not every casting will be perfect. Try several to get the best you can, and be prepared to do some re-sculpting on your casting as you add the back of the head.

6. Figure D (page 66) shows the process using a mold form ring made from a plastic tub. Here, instead of using a piece of Styrofoam, I have placed the heads in a glass baking dish filled with sand. The sand is covered with plastic kitchen wrap to keep it from getting into the mold material and plaster.

THE SIMPLE LATEX MOLD

Liquid latex for making craft molds is usually available in pint or quart cans at craft suppliers. The process for making the mold is exactly the same as for the elasticon mold except that it requires many coats of the material to be painted on and dried between each coat. As craft latex is often more fragile than other rubber materials, filler material such as cheesecloth is often added to a wet coat to keep the latex from tearing when it is lifted away from the casting. Although the material is somewhat smelly and the process time-consuming, it allows the home craftsman an easy way to make a mold of an undercut sculpture.

B Layer of string and cheesecloth for reinforcement

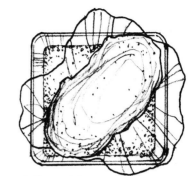

C Plaster built over latex

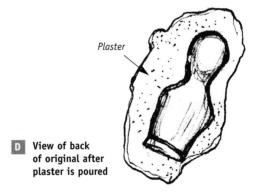

Plaster

D View of back of original after plaster is poured

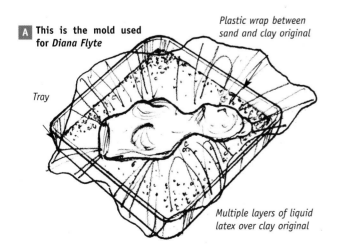

A This is the mold used for *Diana Flyte*

Plastic wrap between sand and clay original

Tray

Multiple layers of liquid latex over clay original

The series of drawings at left and above shows how I made a mold of the original sculpted torso for the figure called *Diana Flyte* (page 68). In this case I painted liquid latex over the original sculpture. This is more economical for larger forms. Several coats must be applied, and each coat must dry thoroughly before the next is applied. As liquid latex is not as strong a material as elasticon, after applying six or eight coats I use a layer of wet cheesecloth to keep the material from tearing later on. Edges can be reinforced by laying a string around the original and painting the latex over the string. Figure A shows the original sculpture laying in a bed of sand covered with plastic kitchen wrap. The figure is buried to a line that evenly divides the back from the front.

Figure B shows the application of plaster to make a "clamshell" mold jacket.

If I want to make a two-piece mold, I would turn the original in its plaster jacket over in the sand bed so the back was exposed and repeat the process of applying liquid latex and plaster. Figure C shows the original with the latex mold and plaster jacket turned showing the back view.

Diana Flyte by Susanna Oroyan, 20", paperclay torso.
Photo by W. Don Smith

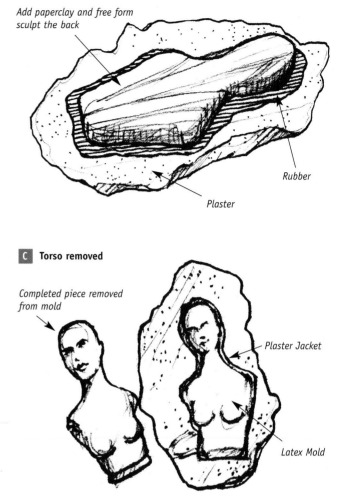

Add paperclay and free form sculpt the back

Rubber

Plaster

C **Torso removed**

Completed piece removed from mold

Plaster Jacket

Latex Mold

A **Making a copy**

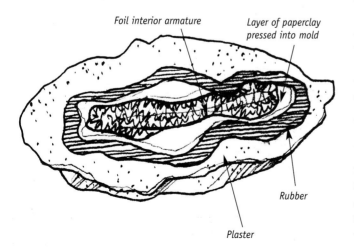

Foil interior armature

Layer of paperclay pressed into mold

Rubber

Plaster

This series of drawings shows the process of making a copy using the finished mold. Figure A shows the plaster jacket containing the latex mold filled with casting material, which in this case is paperclay. A roll of crushed foil can be pressed into the paperclay to form an armature. Also, with foil, less paperclay is used and drying time is shortened. If the foil is brought to the bottom of the figure (waist), it can later be pulled out to make a hollow figure.

Figure B shows paperclay being hand built to form the back of the figure. If a two-piece (back and front) mold has been made, the back mold would be laid over it and pressed down to form the back of the figure, and thus a whole torso.

Figure C shows the cast torso removed from the mold. Heads, torsos, or body parts cast from molds like these are rarely perfect. These processes allow the home-studio doll maker to shortcut sculpting time when making multiples of a figure. You will have to do some re-sculpting and clean-up, but it will involve far less time than sculpting another whole original.

THE RTV MOLD

Another type of rubber mold is made with RTV (a type of silicon rubber). Again, these molds are flexible, allow easy casting of undercut sculpture, and are used for casting materials that do not require the draw of a porous plaster mold. The thickness of the poured mold makes it very firm, and eliminates the need for a plaster jacket. Many dollmakers are now investigating the use of RTV molds for casting edition work in plastics, often referred to as "cold cast porcelain" or "resin" editions. The major difference between using the pourable silicon material and the elasticon process outlined previously is that the pourable material will require a mold form with a wall to contain the liquid.

As with the elasticon, the liquid RTV base is mixed with a catalyst and poured over the model. This mold material takes every surface mark or impression on the original, so it is important to have a clean model. Polymer clay and plasticine clay originals will also require a coating of clear acrylic spray to keep the clay from interacting with the rubber material. When making two-part molds with deep impressions, give care to the placement of pouring gates and sprues that direct the flow of the liquid to all parts of the mold; these have to be trimmed off the finished cast. You might consider the application of a release agent and the use of a vacuum pump.

The process need not be as complicated as it sounds. Many home-based craftsmen are able to make quite satisfactory molds on the kitchen counter using paper cups and bowls for mold forms. For example, you could take your original doll-head sculpture (with a neck or neck-like extension), glue it to the bottom of a paper cup, mix the RTV and its catalyst, and pour the mix into the cup covering the head. When the mold material has set, the cup is torn away, a slice is made in the RTV mold from the back of the head to the neck opening, and the original pops out. For pouring the liquid resin (or wax), the back slit is temporarily sealed, the neck opening becomes the pouring hole, and the mold opens like a book at the back slit to pop out the castings. The casting resin is available in flesh tones; some artists add depth by using make-up to tint the surface, or they paint it with acrylics.

Don't Mess With Me Today, I'm Really Wired
by June Goodnow, 21", Cernit, cloth body over wire armature. Photo by Gerald Chernicoff

WAX RECIPE

■ There are a number of recipes for tooling wax. Tooling wax differs from ordinary candle wax or paraffin in that it is made to be harder and opaque. A typical formula might consist of 800 grams of paraffin or microcrystalline (brown or yellow), 140 grams beeswax (white or yellow), 60 grams carnauba which adds hardness, and 800 grams of talc to make the material opaque. Most of these materials can be obtained from either art or sculpture suppliers. If you wish to experiment, hard waxes are also available from jewelry and dental suppliers. The wax model can be sculpted by addition and subtraction, sanded, carved, and polished. Most professionals who create waxes for production molds use very expensive heated waxing tools and burnishing equipment. You might be able to achieve satisfactory effects with wood burning tools, an alcohol lamp, and burnishing wheels collected from art and jewelry supplies.

THE MOLD AND THE DESIGN PROCESS

Every figure you see in this book evolved through a design process. Some artists are very meticulous in experimenting and making decisions at every step; some more or less add, subtract, and push the materials together. For both types, whatever they do, they do it until "it looks right." The ability to make molds is a great help in the design process in an effort to get "that look," as in the creation of the final edition.

Here, designer Erin Libby shares some of the many steps she took in developing her original copyrighted character figure "PinPon." Erin's experience in working for most of the major toy companies, both in-house and as free-lance designer, is evident in the methods she uses to combine practical technical engineering processes with the final "look" of the character. As you can see, the initial step of making a mold from the original clay sculpture for casting wax is most useful. Each wax casting becomes a sketch pad for testing a different version without having to re-sculpt an entire original. When the final decisions have been made, a refined wax model is cast and sent to the mold maker, who uses it to make production molds. Although Erin's ultimate goal was to cast an edition in resin, she also used her wax models to make molds for casting porcelain versions...to see how they would look as well.

"PinPon is not a single doll, rather an image (or several images) generated from a single concept." But what is the concept? Erin begins to sketch.
"PinPon started with a review of conventional, all too familiar dolls. He began to take on the look of what I wanted once I had drawn what I did not want. Stance became as critical as gesture. I played with foot size and shoes."

"Shoes have been an ordeal. The notion was a cross between Louis the XIV and Victorian. Here is the wax start in front of a sketch." Photo by Betty Weitzenkamp

"I wanted posability, and my first choice was to use a bean bag approach for the body." Photo by Betty Weitzenkamp

"The rough head was painted in acrylic as a color swatch for choosing resin color." Photo by Erin Libby

"Fabric choice and color were issues. I found rayon print more flexible than velvet." Photo by Erin Libby

The profile view shows PinPon as he went to be molded in rubber. The name PinPon had not yet been selected. Photo by Betty Weitzenkamp

Three versions of PinPon by Erin Libby made in resin. Photos by D. Scherrer

Armatures: The Inside Story

The more you know about how things work, the better you will be able to choose the best solutions. Because the doll designer's biggest set of problems involve weight, balance, and pose, you need to consider the use of armatures—the interior structures that provide strength and flexibility—for the figure.

An armature, in the general sense of the term, is any structure that is put inside of something to give it strength and support. For instance, the beams in a house form its armature, and, more apropos to doll making, the bones in the human body form its armature.

As we all know, the human body is a masterpiece of engineering. Nearly a hundred bones from teeny tiny to two feet long are assembled in a complex structure held together by an even more incredible structure of joints, muscles, and tendons. If we did not have this "armatured" support system, we would be shapeless blobs oozing around on the ground. We just could not hold ourselves in any upright position against the great pressures of our planet's gravity. When we are tired, we sag and ache because our joints and muscles—our "armature"—lack energy to carry on the continuous fight against gravity.

In dollmaking we use armatures to make a doll stand up straight or to allow it to be put in a fixed position against the forces of gravity. For instance, a "raggedy" type cloth doll has no "bones" and "muscles" to hold a sitting or standing position without support. Jointing, another way to provide support through balance, reflects knowledge of the structure of the joints and tendons of the human body.

WIRE

Armatures can be made of almost any material. Doll figures made to stand upright are commonly constructed by a process generally referred to among dollmakers as "wire armature." This implies the use of wire bent into a shape roughly resembling a human skeleton in outline form. Wire is used because it functions as both bone and muscle. Its length and hardness extend the covering material, and its flexibility can be used to set or move the figure in the same way as bones and tendons move the human body. With wire you have "two for one."

Wire use by the maker will vary depending on engineering requirements of a specific design, so before going on with construction we need to take a long look at wire itself.

It's wonderful stuff; indispensable for making figures. There is good evidence that wire has been with us almost as long as man has worked metal and, indeed, seems to be referenced in the Bible. Early wire was made by hammering and turning on an anvil and, in consequence, most lengths were quite short. The process of making wire by drawing seems to have originated around 700 AD. According to records, by 1292 there were eight wire-drawing businesses in Paris, and by the early 1400s there was a wire-drawing guild in London. It's not too surprising to find that wire was used in the early stages of modern dollmaking.

Modern wire is made by drawing or pulling a metal bar about one-half inch in diameter through a succession of dies (holes). Each die pass will reduce the diameter of the wire about 25 percent, and it can be reduced to the thickness of a human hair. Gauge refers to the diameter of the wire, and the larger the number the smaller the wire. Wire can be made from any ductile metal; however, the most common forms are iron, copper, brass, aluminum, gold, silver, and lead. During the drawing process the wire is drawn through a lubricant, which can be powdered soap, tallow, grease, or graphite. These lubricant materials can cause the greasy "rub-off" you feel when you work with wire. When the wire is drawn, the metal grains are naturally put under great stress and confusion. To relieve this stress, and to achieve the most soft and ductile condition for the specific metal, the wire is annealed by heating it to just below the melting point of its metal.

Wire comes in more than ten thousand sizes, types, and finishes from galvanized to coated or enameled. Most artists probably would like to have some of everything "just in case." However, you can get by quite nicely with a few basic types.

TYPES OF WIRE

- **17-gauge electrical fence wire**: *economical, multipurpose. Very nice for making bent wire armatures for figures between 12 and 24 inches in height. This wire is usually found in garden and farm supply stores on large spools. Buy a quarter-mile spool. You will use it.*

- **20- and 24-gauge brass wire**: *Nice finish for exposed wire applications, good for making bent wire armatures for figures 2 to 12 inches in height. Usually found in craft suppliers' jewelry sections.*

- **Aluminum or "sculpture" wire**: *This is very soft and flexible material; also very expensive. Makes an excellent non-rusting armature. Comes in gauges 12 and under.*

- **Coat hanger**: *although it acts more like a rod, it can be bent and used for armatures or structures when strength and static pose are required. Coat hanger wire can also be used to make assembly connections for jointed dolls.*

- **Electrical conduit**: *This is the wire that runs inside walls and is usually composed of several spiraled copper wires encased in rubber or plastic coating. Very good for constructing figures from 24 inches to life-size. Often used for smaller figures, but the same effect can be achieved, more economically, by doubling 16- or 17-gauge wire.*

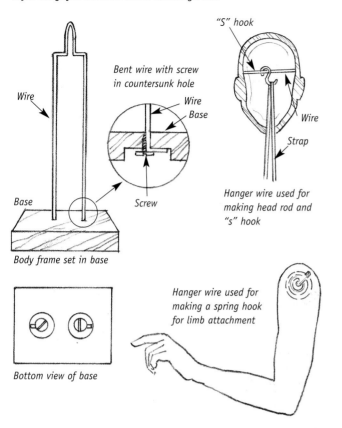

A few things you can make with a coat hanger rod:

Wire

Base

Body frame set in base

Bent wire with screw in countersunk hole

Wire Base

Screw

"S" hook

Wire

Strap

Hanger wire used for making head rod and "s" hook

Bottom view of base

Hanger wire used for making a spring hook for limb attachment

- **Pipe cleaners/chenille**: *fibers are twisted onto the wire to give it a soft body. Useful for making small figure armatures or hand armatures.*

- **Beading wire**: *30-gauge and higher. Use more like sewing thread.*

Wire to avoid: baling wire and any coated wire where lubricant can come off on your fingers or figure. Look for galvanized wire if rust might be a problem. Telephone wire is colorful and fine, as is copper wire, but, in my experience neither have the strength necessary for constructing a good stand-up body. Floral wire, which comes in 18-inch lengths, is strong but the joining required usually defeats the value of continuous run bent wire. Plane and train model suppliers usually carry a selection of metal rods. Most figure makers will find it handy to have a selection of hollow brass tubing. It can be used for jointing and/or for building stand supports for figures. Look to see what else might be handy for your work when shopping at the model supplier.

Wire also comes in mesh grid patterns such as fencing and screening. Most screen material is coated with plastic, which limits its ability to be bent for sculptural purposes. Uncoated metal screening will usually rust. Fine grid fencing materials—¼ inch to 1 inch (chicken wire or vent covering material)—are useful when crushed to build out larger forms.

WIRE PHYSICS

Most dollmakers would snort at the idea of doing physics or engineering, yet a good figure maker will know a great deal about what works and what won't with any material. With wire there are four important factors to consider: The first is what happens when you twist wire—you create a spring, and springs are not going to give you the necessary strength. In doing research some years back, I was surprised to find that most dollmaking books showed twisted wire armatures (and just as often they did not include correct bends for hips and shoulders). If you take two pieces of wire and twist them with your hands only, one wire will be twisted around the other, which stays fairly straight. This means that even if two wires are used, you are only getting half the strength of one. If you can hook a loop of wire to a fixed peg and twist with great strength, you can get an equal bend on each wire and, therefore, maximum strength. Most dollmakers don't have the strength or the tools. Keep your wires parallel and twist over them only if you want additional grip or to tuck in ends.

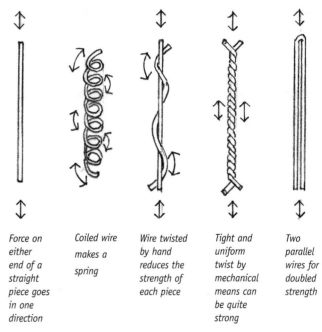

Force on either end of a straight piece goes in one direction

Coiled wire makes a spring

Wire twisted by hand reduces the strength of each piece

Tight and uniform twist by mechanical means can be quite strong

Two parallel wires for doubled strength

The second factor has to do with anatomy. The purpose of a wire armature is defeated if the proper shaping is not done to simulate hip and shoulder. An inverted "V" to form the legs will not resist gravity. The figure will do splits when any weight or force like a sculpted head or stuffed body is applied. And, of course, if a figure doesn't have shoulders that stick out beyond the hips, it is anatomically incorrect. At the very least, you will have a nasty time getting clothing to look right on it.

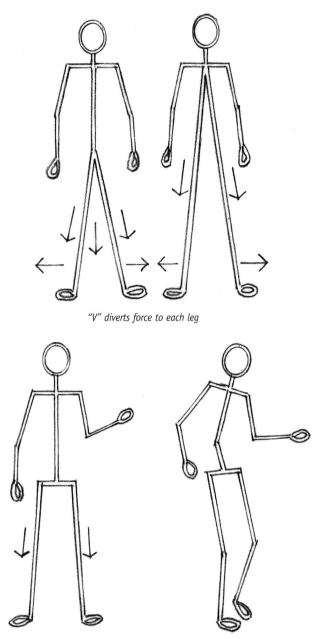

"V" diverts force to each leg

Force directed straight down in anatomically correct armature; also, figure stands on its own two feet

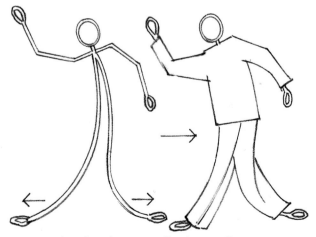

A poorly made armature will make a poor figure

The third factor concerns material integrity and is specific to building clay on wire armatures. Stop to consider what the wire is doing inside the sculpted material. Its presence is interrupting the molecular integrity of the sculpture material. All sculpting materials work by the bonding and fusing of particles of like material to like material. If a second material (the wire) runs through it, the bonding is stopped. The wire itself has no ability to fuse with sculpture material. So the wire forms a core, sometimes a loose or hollow core, through the middle of the sculpted part. If the particles of the sculpture material are able to reach around the wire, they will provide the strength you want. The smaller the amount of sculpture material, the less strong the part is likely to be. This is especially true in the case of hand/finger armatures in direct sculpted figures.

Molecules dried or cured fuse together. *Wire through molecules interrupts fusion.* *Wire movement creates a hollow core.*

The final consideration is that all armatures and armatured figures should stand by themselves. If they don't, work on position and balance until they do.

WIRE ANATOMY

The prime aesthetic principle of an armature deals with how the figure will look when it is finished. In order for the form to look "believably humanoid" when the armature is buried in material or covered with a costume, the armature must reflect generally correct anatomical proportions. The body must look like it could walk or move like a human. Even if it will never be moved, the joints should be properly placed. This means that the arms hang free from the shoulders and outside of the hips, and that there is space between the hips so the legs can move in parallel. The wrists, ankles, and waist should also be narrower than their surroundings. It means that elbows and knees are given their correct "bulges." You also need to remember that no matter how much flesh may cover a body, the points of the major joint bones will also be visible. Regardless of the size, costume, or position of your figure, the basic layout for any armature must conform to the human shape to be successful.

An armature is not just something to hold up a doll; it has to work like a simplified human skeleton with muscles and tendons. Obviously, making an armature involves a good understanding and use of human body mechanics as well as the properties of the armature material. As you work with the various armature materials, you will find those that have the desired properties. A good anatomy reference will help you understand how to position the joints and proportion the final shape.

TYPICAL ARMATURE FORMS

SINGLE WIRE

A single armature is made with one or two fairly thick pieces of wire or metal rod. The most common material is wire from wire coat hangers. This type of armature is usually made to create a finished figure that will be fixed in a specific position. A solid base of wood or modeled material such as plaster is often used as a permanent base for this type of figure.

With a single armature, often only heads, hands, and feet will show. The body might be left in a rough state or given just enough padding with paper, fabric, or batting material to provide the desired shape. In a single wire armature, the arms may or may not be armatured and, if they are, the maker has the option of attaching arm wires to the torso or leaving them loose.

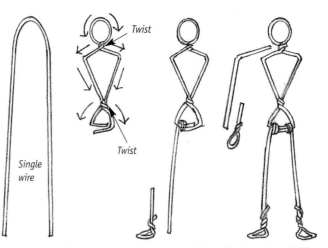

Twist

Twist

Single wire

A variation on the single wire armature successfully used by John Darcy Noble for his paper sculpture maquettes.

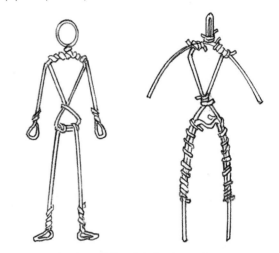

Another variation of single wire armature

The Green Man by John Darcy Noble, 12", Super Sculpey, washi paper. Photo by John Darcy Noble

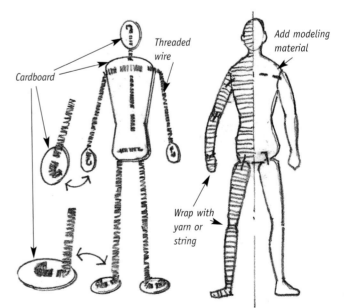

Threaded wire

Cardboard

Add modeling material

Wrap with yarn or string

Single wire armature made with cardboard torso, head, hands, and feet. Wire is threaded through the cardboard.

The cardboard and wire armature can be padded out by wrapping with yarn or string, or material may be modeled on it.

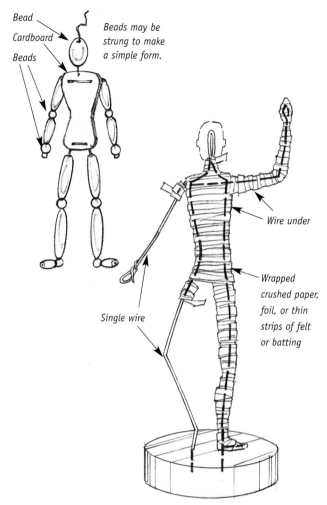

Bead

Cardboard

Beads

Beads may be strung to make a simple form.

Wire under

Single wire

Wrapped crushed paper, foil, or thin strips of felt or batting

A single wire may be posed and wrapped with crushed paper, foil, or thin strips of felt or batting and finally covered with fabric.

DOUBLE WIRE

The form I refer to as the "M" or "W" method is the one I use most when inserting an armature into a cloth body that will be positioned for a particular pose. A modified version of this form is used when assembling separately sculpted parts. You can use 16- or 17-gauge (electrical fence) wire for figures from 12 to 24 inches. For figures over 20 inches, you might want to make a double run of wire for added strength. For figures smaller than 12 inches, you can use 20-gauge wire as found in the jewelry supplies section in craft stores. Notice that the wires do not cross except when the ends are finally twisted into the torso.

Nova by Thea Newcombe, 17", wrapped wire armature, sculpted cloth-covered face. Photo by W. Don Smith

New Perm (left, copper and brass wire)and *Hazel's Pearls* (right, wire and pearls) by Annie Wylde-Beem. Photo by Barbara Carleton Evans

Jurnee by Elizabeth Harper, 13", and *Wild Woman* (right) by Barbara Carleton Evans, 12", electrical wire and yarn. Photo by Barbara Carleton Evans

Use masking tape to hold the wires together while working. Lay your pieces out on your doll pattern or on a sketch of the finished shape to check their length. Also remember that if your doll is to be stuffed—that is, the armature is first inserted into the cloth body and then stuffing is inserted around the wire—that the stuffing process will widen and shorten the doll somewhat from your pattern pieces. Be prepared to adjust as necessary.

When you have your figure assembled, if it has a flat foot bottom or shoe sole, it should be able to stand by itself! Move it around until it does. It will even stand on one leg, or stand with one leg extended away from its body, although you might have to weight its "bottom" a little to get a leg extension to balance.

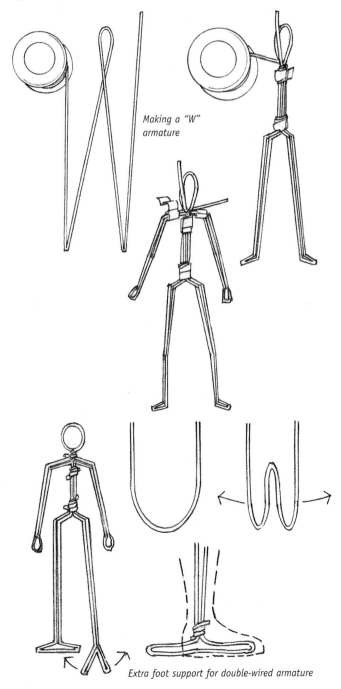

Making a "W" armature

Extra foot support for double-wired armature

ALTERNATE "W"

This method is often seen in European "tourist souvenir" dolls made during the 1930s...and some very expressive pieces can result. Here the wire armature is wrapped rather tightly with thin, firm batting such as is used to make quilted clothing. You can also wrap with string or yarn so the fibers open and flatten. The general body shape is sculpted

during the process of wrapping the wire armature; the finished wrapped armature is almost exactly the shape of the finished form. The figure is then covered by hand sewing pieces of fabric—usually felt—over the limbs. Paper patterns are made by a trial-and-error method of holding soft fabric (such as interfacing) or soft paper (such as a paper napkin) around the figure and cutting away the excess. This was discussed in detail in *Anatomy of a Doll*.

Flapper by Susanna Oroyan, 12", wire armature wrapped with embroidery thread. Photo by W. Don Smith

MODIFIED "M" OR "W" ARMATURE

This armature is used to assemble sculpted parts as discussed on page 84. Arms and legs should have holes for inserting wires. These can be drilled if using paperclay products. If using polymer clays, insert wires in limbs before curing in the oven. In this form, the armature only goes as far as the beginning of the sculpted part(s). This means it is very important to lay out your pieces on a properly proportioned sketch of the finished doll to make sure measurements are to correct scale. When the modified armature is made, the wires extending from the sculpted limbs are run alongside (parallel) of the body armature and taped together. Generally, the completed wire figure is covered with a wrapping of inch-wide strips of quilt batting, yarn, or string for smaller figures. A body of woven cotton, polyester double knit, stockinette knit, or even bathing suit stretch fabric (such as Lycra®) is usually hand sewn over the wrapped armature. The hand sewing allows some darting and needlesculpting to enhance anatomical details such as bust, waistline, elbows, and knees.

SKELETAL

Heavy wire may be used to create a single or double armature, which is then over-wrapped with several layers of thin wire to reflect the human bone structure. This type of armature can be used for direct sculpture as it provides a structural mesh that will hold clay. A similar form of armature is used by Lisa Lichtenfels as a basis for building a musculature of padded stuffing covered with needlesculpted nylon stocking.

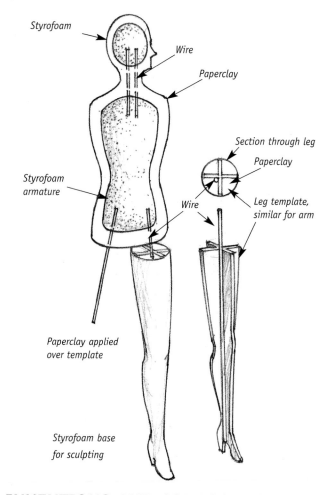

Styrofoam
Wire
Paperclay
Styrofoam armature
Section through leg
Paperclay
Wire
Leg template, similar for arm
Paperclay applied over template
Styrofoam base for sculpting

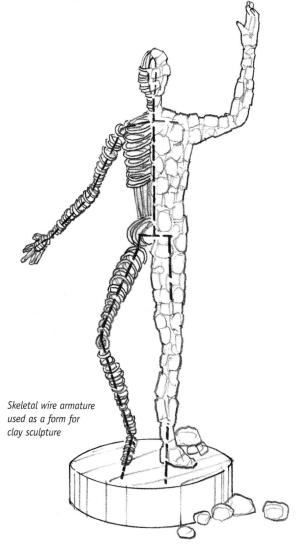

Skeletal wire armature used as a form for clay sculpture

CARVED OR ASSEMBLED STYROFOAM HEAD ARMATURES

These are often used for needlesculpted figures. Styrofoam is never to be used with polymer clays as it can give off toxic vapors when heated. A full skull can be sculpted or a framework of foam core can be made.

Many dollmakers favor sculpting over a styrofoam base using a template to form the leg armature. The method shown (above right) is used by Robert Doucette. Here paperclay is sculpted over styrofoam cores. The head and body are done separately and joined by wires. The leg is sculpted over a cardboard or balsa template for accuracy and strength.

INVENTIONS AND COMPOSITES

Although wire is the most common form of armature, there are other ways of making your figure stand up, pose, or be solid. An armature can be made of anything you have that will work.

Many dollmakers, for instance, have found that working with clays on wire armatures is "slippery." The material has no way of gripping the smooth wire surface. One way to get around slippage is to wrap the wire armature with a layer of aluminum foil.

Double armatures: Another way is to create a double armature—you model a thin, basic "string" armature of the same clay. This is dried or cured and then a second layer is applied for the finished surface. Artists who work with paperclay find that they can achieve a solid stickable sculpture base by making a string armature or set of "bones" out of the heavier and more coarse Celluclay material. Since Celluclay and paperclay dry at various rates, any bones made of Celluclay need to be thoroughly dry before adding paperclay material. Be sure to cover Celluclay completely as it is very difficult to sand or carve when dry. The same can be done with the oven curing clays in a cook add-on and cook again process.

Pop-bead assemblies: Still another type of armature is the commercially produced "pop-bead" assembly. In this type a body form made of plastic beads is purchased for insertion into a stuffed cloth body. Size can be adjusted by popping off or adding on more beads. The swivel action of the socket connection allows the figure to be posed in any position. The size of the beads, however, makes this form best in larger dolls and teddy bears—usually figures over 15 inches and/or fairly "chubby" in body shape. The pop-bead armatures are successfully used in assembling porcelain parts on cloth bodies.

In the end, all dollmakers adapt and invent to suit a particular need or want. This involves problem solving, and problem solving begins with asking questions.

WORKING ARMATURES

Up to this point, I have discussed armatures that are permanently fixed inside the finished doll. Many of us have also picked up basic armature information from art studio methods for fine art sculpture in metals and fired clays. The armatures used for this kind of art work are often temporary. They are made to hold up the original sculpture until it reaches a point where a mold can be made for casting the final, usually hollow, product. Since at least half of all dollmakers work in modeled clay materials, a quick look at working armatures might be useful.

In this type of working armature a full and correctly proportioned wire armature is made for the whole figure. The figure is sculpted as a whole, which allows the artist to see the relationships between various areas. It allows for instant "eyeball" correction. Many times fine sculptors fail in their finished figures because they sculpt the parts separately and have difficulty getting scale and proportion correct for the whole figure. If a full armature can be made, and the sculpture done as a whole, then the sculpture can be cut apart. Use a hacksaw to cut through wire and sculpted material. Cut where joints are needed or cut away excess clay if a fabric body is to be made. Yes, this does mess up the ends of the parts. You will need to resculpt a bit after cutting. A single-wire armature can be made for wax sculpture, and an "M" or double-wire armature, over-wrapped with finer wire, will provide a "tooth" for applying clay.

Wire and Mesh: A shortcut method for creating a form for needlesculpting can be done by constructing a fixed form of wire covered with mesh. This would be applicable if a large (over 30-inch) or life-size figure was desired. Wire and mesh armatures can also be used for sculpting figures that are to be cast in molds—usually larger fixed figure pieces.

Wire/mesh and wet newspaper armatures: These can be used for portrait bust and torso sculpture with water-based ceramic clays. When the sculpture is complete, the head is cut in half and the wire frame removed. The paper is peeled away, leaving two hollow halves which may be joined with wet clay and fired.

HAND-HELD

A plain dowel stick is best if a head is to be sculpted separately. This allows the sculptor to turn the head around, upside down, etc., to check for correct balance and smoothness. Sculpting on a fixed armature is very good for proportioning, but requires the artist to work extra hard and be alert to optical illusions and tricks the brain will play. For instance, when you look at a figure face-on or face-to-face, your brain will identify it as a human figure or face. Your brain sees humans all the time and does not really register "perfection" when it does; it just accepts and names what it sees. If a head or figure is turned upside down, your brain cannot readily identify or name it. It just sees a shape, so it will tell you (if you ask!) that one side is too big or too high. Correcting is much easier when the figure can be moved.

Sculpture tends to be unbalanced because we use a dominant hand that works more efficiently on the side of the figure it is closest to. The same is true with your dominant eye, which is often the same side as your handedness. The result is "slide," or a tendency for the nondominant side to recede more radically. The bossiness of your dominant hand and/or eye keeps you from seeing this imbalance. If you look at your work reflected in a mirror, your dominant eye will see the other—possibly poor—side of the sculpture. A mirror check can often be a ghastly shock. Remember, the viewer's hand, eyes, and brains may not be wired the same as yours for dominance...he or she might see imbalances as more immediate and glaring than you do.

Archangel Raphael and Tobias by Karan A. Schneider, 21", Cernit with wire and soft body. Photo by Studio Rossi Inc.

CHECKING SCULPTURE

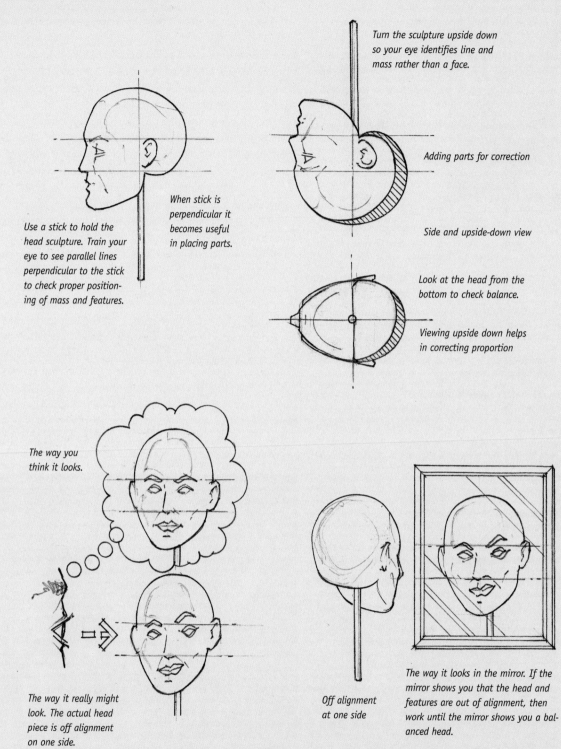

Turn the sculpture upside down so your eye identifies line and mass rather than a face.

Adding parts for correction

Use a stick to hold the head sculpture. Train your eye to see parallel lines perpendicular to the stick to check proper positioning of mass and features.

When stick is perpendicular it becomes useful in placing parts.

Side and upside-down view

Look at the head from the bottom to check balance.

Viewing upside down helps in correcting proportion

The way you think it looks.

The way it really might look. The actual head piece is off alignment on one side.

Off alignment at one side

The way it looks in the mirror. If the mirror shows you that the head and features are out of alignment, then work until the mirror shows you a balanced head.

Note: Both the full-figure sculpture and the sand-sock method that follow are best done on a turntable with a mirror behind. Sculptor's turntables are available, but the type used for kitchen cupboard storage (small spice rack type) will work just as well.

SAND SOCK

When a figure is made hollow to eliminate weight or to allow for jointing, the clay material can be modeled over a sock filled with sand. In modeling paperclay, for instance, I will fill the sock over a dowel and use tape to contour the narrowing at the neck or to create a waist. To make the sock "non-stick" I add a layer of crushed kitchen foil. After the sculpture is finished and at least partly dry, I "pull the plug" on the sock, drain the sand, and use pliers to gently pull out the foil. The figure can be further hollowed by scraping out damp clay from the inside. The

result is a torso that is lightweight and can accept a wired cloth leg/hip assembly. In this process the head is not attached to the body while sculpting the majority of the body. It does, however, sit on the neck so the head and body can be sculpted with smooth and proportionate lines. It is taken off and on to get the benefit of the hand-held sculpting, and fixed when both parts are satisfactorily sculpted. The head can be attached by a joint through the neck or it can be joined to the body with wet clay and sculpted to make a solid, immovable connection.

Sand sock can also be used for head-only sculpture and with water-based ceramic clays.

Sand Sock for Head Sculpture and Torso

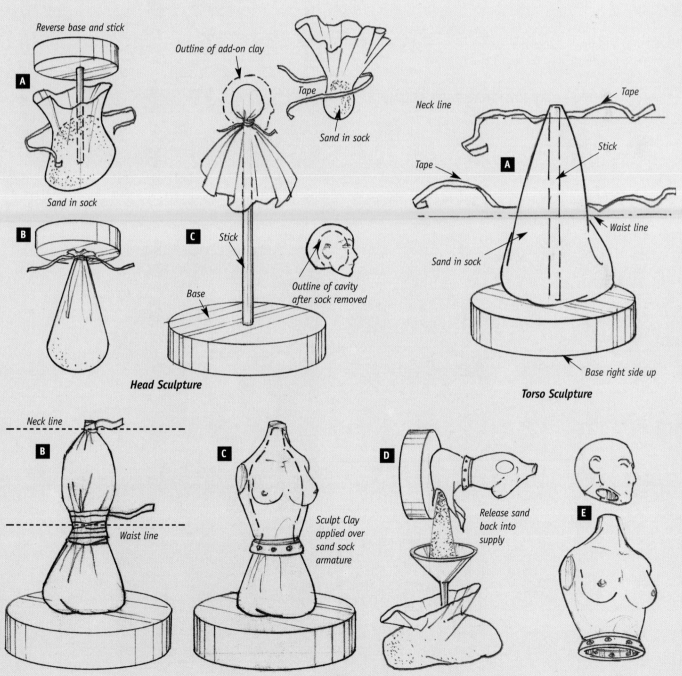

Head Sculpture

Torso Sculpture

Torso Sculpture

Assemblies

As opposed to a figure created from one material (such as carved wood or stuffed cloth), I define an assembly as a figure that was constructed using two or more materials or methods. The most common assembly is a wire-armatured cloth body combined with hard sculpted parts—porcelain, resin, polymer, or paperclay. If the design hasn't been outlined you must have had a question—Now what do I do to make this a figure I can costume and finish? Before you can go any further, you need to choose a form (back to design) and finish your sculpture so it can be assembled. As you can see, this will require making appropriate holes, grooving parts so a cloth body can be attached, and inserting wires which are then attached to a center wire armature.

Traditionally, fired ceramic dolls were assembled on stuffed cloth bodies like the figure below.

Hannah Rose variations by Susan Dunham, 19", limited edition, porcelain with wood cage, inset jewels. Photo by Susan Dunham

TRADITIONAL BODY ASSEMBLY

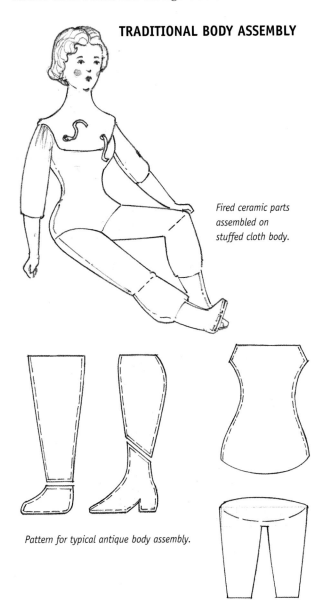

Fired ceramic parts assembled on stuffed cloth body.

Pattern for typical antique body assembly.

Virgin Mary: The Conception by Antonette Cely, 18", paperclay over fabric on wood frame. Photo by Don B. Cely

SCULPTURE MECHANICS

No matter how organized we want to be in designing, more often we find ourselves with an interesting head and no idea in the world how to put it together to make a figure.

If you have a head sculpture that looks promising, the first thing to do is figure out what sort of a body it will need. This decision needs to be made before the material is cured, dried, or painted. Let's assume you have the head. Now what?

If you have not begun with a sketch or used a template, you need to make one now to fit your figure. Then, you need to sculpt the feet and legs.

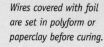

Wires covered with foil are set in polyform or paperclay before curing.

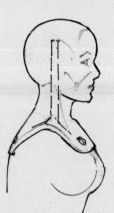

Neck grooved to receive body fabric

Breastplate with holes for sewing or tying to soft body

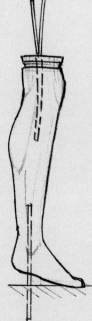

Wires extending from cured sculpture.

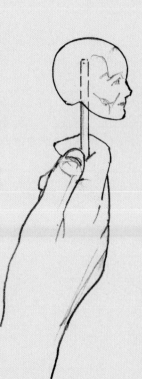

Mah Jong Madness by Susanna Oroyan, 20" seated, paperclay head and limbs on soft cloth body. Photo by W. Don Smith

Wire armature extending through the foot to form support.

A foot sculpted to wear a high heel.

A foot drilled to fit over a rod set into a base.

PRE-WIRED PARTS

This is the typical method for joining sculpted parts that will be assembled on a wire armature. You should have made grooves in sculpted polymer or ceramic before curing. Paperclay can be grooved after drying, if material is at least ³/₈-inch thick.

SCULPTING

1. Sculpt hands to wrist if costume will cover arms. This allows greater movement in positioning the arm.

2. Check to make sure the hands will realistically hold an object if that is part of your design.

3. If the foot is to have a shoe, sculpt the foot as a shoe last.

4. Sculpt the leg to give maximum strength for standing—at least to the knee.

5. Make holes and groove all parts when clay is soft. Grooves need to be deep and wide enough to hold a double thickness of body fabric.

6. Insert wires before curing.

7. Make holes in the feet if the body is to be inserted into a base.

ASSEMBLING

1. Use the diagram as a guide to make a modified wire armature. Use your full-figure sketch or a proportional body drawing as a guide for laying out the wire (not shown). The wire bends in this armature will be made so they meet the end of the limb.

2. Lay wires extending from limbs along side of body wires. Tape wires together.

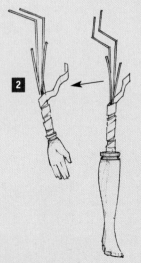

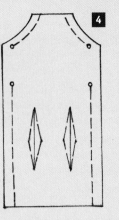

3. Wrap entire body with strips of quilt batting or felt. This creates a very strong body (not shown).

4. Design, cut, and sew body torso from cloth. Add darts to body as necessary for design.

5. Bend arms up and slip fabric body over neck wires as if putting on a shirt. Adjust body over wrapping and stuff firmly to fill out as necessary.

6. If arm and leg parts are wide enough to slip over hands and feet, follow inserting steps shown below.

7. If it is not possible to make a gathered turn, pin fabric around limb and hand stitch a seam from wrist to shoulder and/or from leg top to hip. When seam is hand sewn, turn raw edges under at limb ends and gather (not shown).

8. Pose arms and stuff as needed to achieve sharp elbow. Insert stuffing at shoulder top, gather fabric arm top, and hand stitch to body. Be sure shoulder makes a sharp angle.

9. Stuff legs as necessary. Insert extra stuffing to create a knee if limb ends below knee.

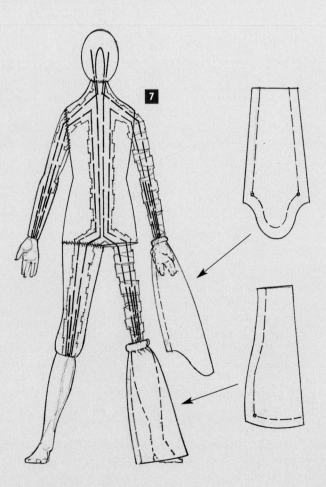

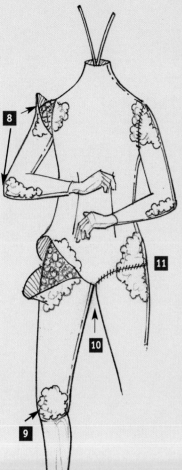

10. Sew body together at center bottom to form crotch.

11. Bring leg tops up over body fabric, turn under, pin to hold, and hand stitch to secure.

12. Attaching the head: Bend the wire to fit it in the hole in the head, push head down so the neck groove is inside body opening. Gather to close. Alternate: Gather head to separate piece of fabric. Slip head over neck wires and hand stitch fabric to body.

Option: If using a breastplate, apply white glue to body top, slip head over wire.

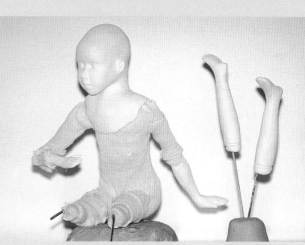

Jennifer by Marleen Engeler, 15", stoneclay. Clay parts being assembled with wire and covered with cloth. Photos by Marleen Engeler

Jennifer finished

BODY CONSTRUCTED FOR A SPECIAL SHAPE

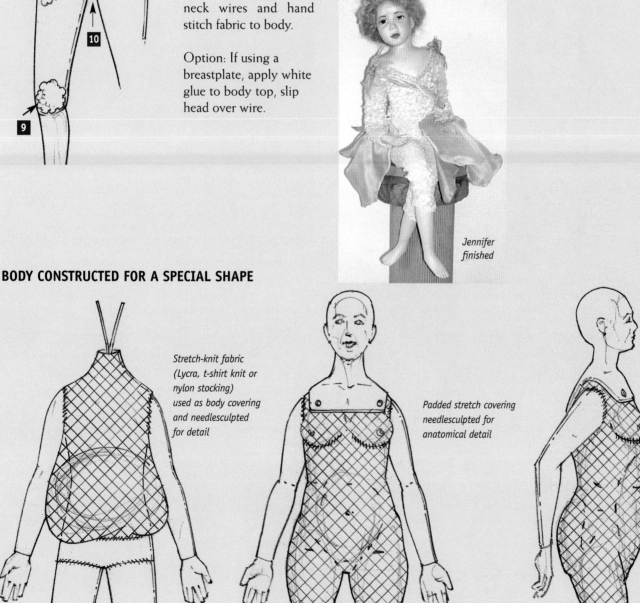

Stretch-knit fabric (Lycra, t-shirt knit or nylon stocking) used as body covering and needlesculpted for detail

Padded stretch covering needlesculpted for anatomical detail

DEVELOPING SCULPTURE AND POSE

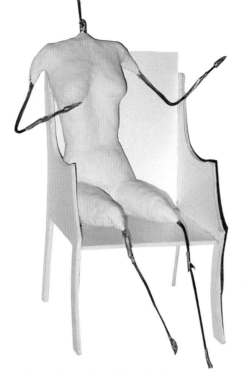

Cleopatra by Sandra Wright Justiss, in progress. Paperclay being applied to wire armature and posed to fit frame of chair. Photo by Sandra Wright Justiss

Cleopatra with finished chair. Collar is made of authentic mummybeads that are at least 2600 years old. Photo by Sandra Wright Justiss

Checker Players by Betsey Baker, 12"x 14", Super Sculpey and La Doll. The artist begins her figures by making a wire armature and posing it to fit the framework of the proposed setting furniture. Photos by Betsey Baker

As the work progresses, limbs are sculpted of Super Sculpey and the furniture is covered with Celluclay.

The finished group.

A TAILORED FABRIC BODY

Even though Mary Ellen Frank makes figures dressed in the loose costumes of the Arctic, she needed to create a very specific body design in order to make the clothes look like they were covering real bodies. Here is one version she created for a sitting figure.

Anna and Alice, by Mary Ellen Frank, NIADA, 14 ¹/₂" and 10", carved birch heads, cloth needlesculpted and jointed bodies. Photos by Mary Ellen Frank

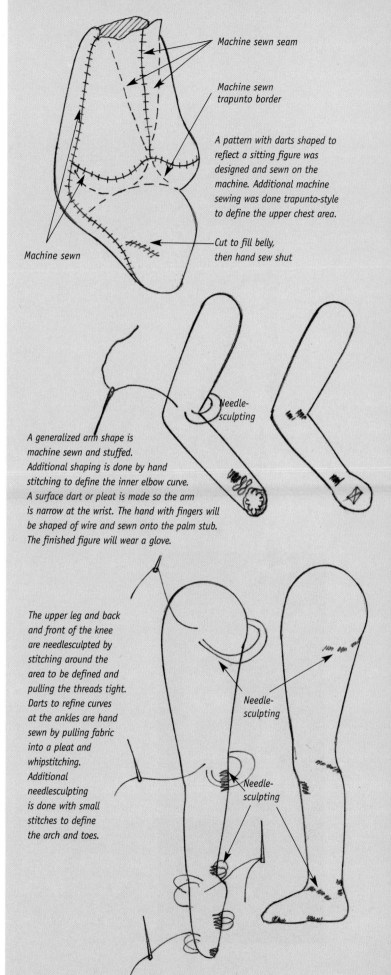

Machine sewn seam

Machine sewn trapunto border

A pattern with darts shaped to reflect a sitting figure was designed and sewn on the machine. Additional machine sewing was done trapunto-style to define the upper chest area.

Machine sewn

Cut to fill belly, then hand sew shut

A generalized arm shape is machine sewn and stuffed. Additional shaping is done by hand stitching to define the inner elbow curve. A surface dart or pleat is made so the arm is narrow at the wrist. The hand with fingers will be shaped of wire and sewn onto the palm stub. The finished figure will wear a glove.

Needle-sculpting

The upper leg and back and front of the knee are needlesculpted by stitching around the area to be defined and pulling the threads tight. Darts to refine curves at the ankles are hand sewn by pulling fabric into a pleat and whipstitching. Additional needlesculpting is done with small stitches to define the arch and toes.

Needle-sculpting

Needle-sculpting

THE CLOTH BODY AS AN ARMATURE

Working with traditional Japanese dollmaking techniques, Akiko Anzai begins her figure by constructing a very firmly stuffed cloth body. Wires are inserted to help connect the limbs to the body. The limbs are positioned as desired and hand sewn for final attachment. The paperclay feet and head are sculpted directly onto the assembled body. When the sculpture is dry, padding is applied where it is needed. The final layer of "skin" is applied by laying the fabric around the body parts, gluing, then cutting away the excess.

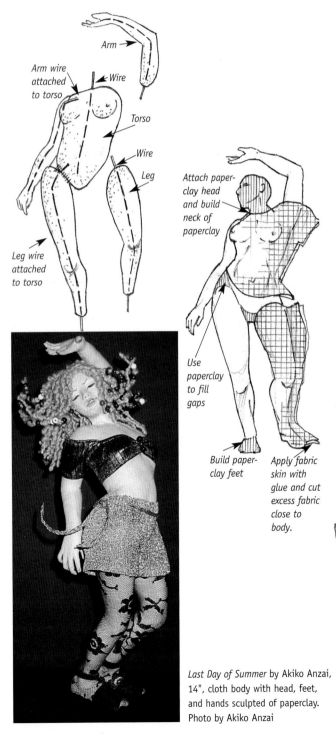

Arm

Arm wire attached to torso

Wire

Torso

Wire

Leg

Leg wire attached to torso

Attach paperclay head and build neck of paperclay

Use paperclay to fill gaps

Build paperclay feet

Apply fabric skin with glue and cut excess fabric close to body.

Last Day of Summer by Akiko Anzai, 14", cloth body with head, feet, and hands sculpted of paperclay. Photo by Akiko Anzai

SCULPTED TORSO/SITTING FIGURE

As it is often difficult to get a costume to fit and drape nicely over a breastplate construction, you might need to sculpt a full torso. The following figures show the attachment of the sand-sock torso to a finished figure. This type of assembly is particularly good for a figure that will sit in either a fixed position or be changeable from sitting to standing supported.

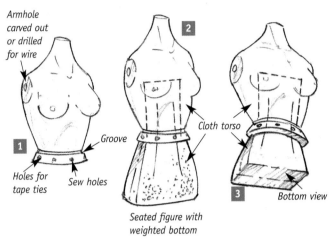

Armhole carved out or drilled for wire

1

2

Groove

Cloth torso

Holes for tape ties

Sew holes

3

Bottom view

Seated figure with weighted bottom

1. The torso is drilled or sculpted to receive the upper arm. A groove is sculpted or carved into the waist to reduce the bulk of a gathered skirt or pleats. Optional holes may be inserted for a tied attachment.

2. An inner torso of stuffed cloth is made and weighted (see weight bag pattern in Cloth chapter, page 127).

3. The sculpted torso is glued to the cloth torso.

4

Straight wire

4. A wire is run through the torso at the shoulder and taped to pre-wired sculpted arms. OR A fully sculpted arm with ball top is hooked to a spring running through the torso at the shoulder.

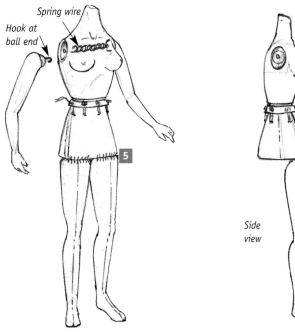

Hook at ball end

Spring wire

5

5

Side view

5. A cloth upper leg is gathered into the groove at the upper part of the sculpted leg, positioned, and sewn to the body at the hip area.
OR
A stuffed or assembled leg can be sewn to the front of the cloth torso to allow the figure to change position.

INSERTED WIRE

If you have designed a cloth figure and want to add a wire armature, use your pattern as a guide.

Lay pattern pieces out with a 1-inch overlap to form an armature guide. The overlap is made to allow for the take-up or widening of the body that will occur when it is stuffed. Construct an "M" armature. Sew body, arms, and legs, leaving openings for stuffing. Insert wire into the body and stuff. Insert wire into limbs and stuff. Hand stitch limb tops to body as in pre-wired parts instructions (page 84).

EXERCISES

Design a figure and outline a construction process that allows two or three different bodies to share one leg or one pair of legs.

How does a cloth surface that has been fully painted for an "oil" effect give the designer a particular set of options for costuming or achieving a unique impression? Can you think of more than one effect that you could achieve?

How would you vary the typical wire armature so it would allow a hollow rod to extend from the leg into a hole in a wood base?

Angel In An Apron by Susanna Oroyan, 24", cloth. Photo by W. Don Smith

La Sylliphede by Scott R. Gray, 12 ½", glass. Photo by Roger Schreiber

COMBINED FIGURE: THE DANCER

We don't always have the leisure to design a figure from the start. *The Dancer* was truly a case of putting parts together. It began with a head and a body that were made for two different lecture demonstrations.

I sculpted a mask of polymer clay, covered it with crinkle gauze, set in plastic eyes, and painted the features with acrylics. For a demonstration piece, I had sculpted a wire armature body by wrapping it with half-inch strips of felt. Somewhat later I wanted to make a ballerina figure and, on checking proportions, these parts looked like they would work together for my idea. Just to give myself a choice, I sculpted, painted, and covered two more masks. Here are the problem and solution steps that I went through to complete the doll you see.

First, I had to determine a pose, otherwise the costume and needlesculpted details would not reflect the correct anatomy. The positioning of the feet was especially important as this would determine interior details for making the doll stand without external support (always most desirable). The wrapped armature was adjusted until it could stand by itself, taking the weight of the figure on one leg. This meant making sure the supporting leg was straight and the weight of the figure vectored into the one supporting leg in an artistic position. At this point, both legs were undone and re-wrapped to insert a small brass rod that would eventually extend through the foot and shoe into a wood base. Because the edges of the wrapped felt would telegraph through the top layer of gauze, the whole figure had to have an underskin of felt, hand stitched and darted to accentuate the dancer figure and pose.

During this stage, I decided to create a wire-armatured hand with separate fingers. As hand stitching gauze over separate fingers in this scale would be difficult, I decided to machine sew the hand with a layer of gauze between the felt pieces. However, felt was too thick for turning the fingers so a suedecloth of the same color was used instead.

In designing the final body covering, several options were available. The main problem was picking one so the finished covering presented a uniform, minimally seamless look. I needed to choose a gauze skin with seams that would be all hand stitched. I placed my top layer of gauze so the seams fell along the inside of the arm and up the back of the leg like a stocking. A single piece went over the shoulders to cover the upper torso with a seam running from the side over the top of the arm where the costume sleeve would cover it. The neck was wrapped and stitched so the seam fell under the neck ribbon.

Before adding the head, costume and color decisions had to be made. The options were: a white-on-white textured fabric look with the only color the blue of the eyes; or, I could do the figure with lip and cheek color, black hair,

red tutu bodice, and a highly colorful print shawl that picked up the red, black, and pink head details—one bright splash and many little unobtrusive touches.

In the construction of this piece, two other options were briefly considered, rejected, and put in the save-for-another-version pile. They were: an outer skin of lightweight velour, covering the whole body with gauze, and painting it in an "oil painting" effect. Now suppose I wanted to show all three versions in one piece? I would have had to figure out construction and pose that would allow three torsos to be blended into the one supporting leg.

In this sort of design-as-you-go process at each step in the construction process—or before—the construction has to be coordinated with both the design of the particular part and its relation to the final, completed look. Each step is an "if I do this, then what happens?" process that must be visualized to the completion of the figure. The same has to happen in a predetermined design. You must visualize the exact final effect, down through all the layers, to know exactly what will be necessary to get the effect you know you want.

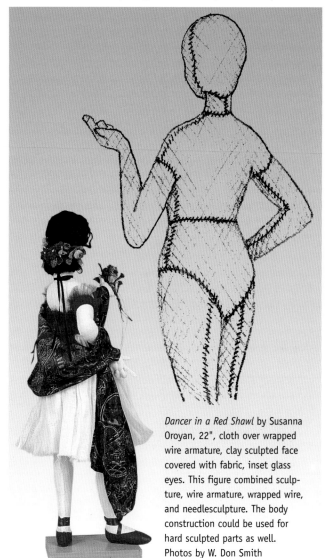

Dancer in a Red Shawl by Susanna Oroyan, 22", cloth over wrapped wire armature, clay sculpted face covered with fabric, inset glass eyes. This figure combined sculpture, wire armature, wrapped wire, and needlesculpture. The body construction could be used for hard sculpted parts as well. Photos by W. Don Smith

LARGE AND SMALL FIGURES

Small scale figures are fascinating because we are just simply amazed that our large hands can work with tiny parts. Large figures are equally fascinating because they look like us.

In creating small scale figures—usually miniature scale, which is one inch to one foot—the major consideration is shrinkage. When you do a miniature scale figure, you always have to bear in mind that to be successful, all parts have to shrink uniformly. Often, this means that tiny things in real human scale will shrink to be microscopic or invisible in the figure. Consider how fine a human hair is: if it is reduced in scale six times, you wouldn't be able to see it. For the maker, this means being very sure that materials, patterns, and textures chosen reflect that reduction.

When you construct large figures—usually equal to human proportion—the major consideration is weight. Light as it is, the amount of stuffing it would take to fill a six-foot tall figure would make it extremely heavy and unwieldy. For basic floppy figures, the problem can be solved by making bags or pillow shapes of shredded foam rubber or Styrofoam cookies to put inside cloth bodies. Since these materials have a tendency to telegraph their rough surfaces, the bags need to be covered over with stuffing material to achieve a smooth surface look. Sheets of foam rubber mattress material might also be used. Mattress material needs to be covered tightly to eliminate show-through of cut/clipped edges.

Commedia del Arte by Ellen Rixford, 5', paper maché, foam, wood, metal, motors, fabric. Photo by Ellen Rixford

Vincent and Prudence by Betsy Baker, 60" and 64". Heads and hands for these life-sized figures were sculpted of air-drying Celluclay and mounted on a body constructed of heavy-duty wire padded out with blanket strips, sculpted with polyester filling, and covered with stretch fabric. Photo by Betsy Baker

Friends by Dorothy Hoskins, 5", Super Sculpey. Photo by Pauline Chamness

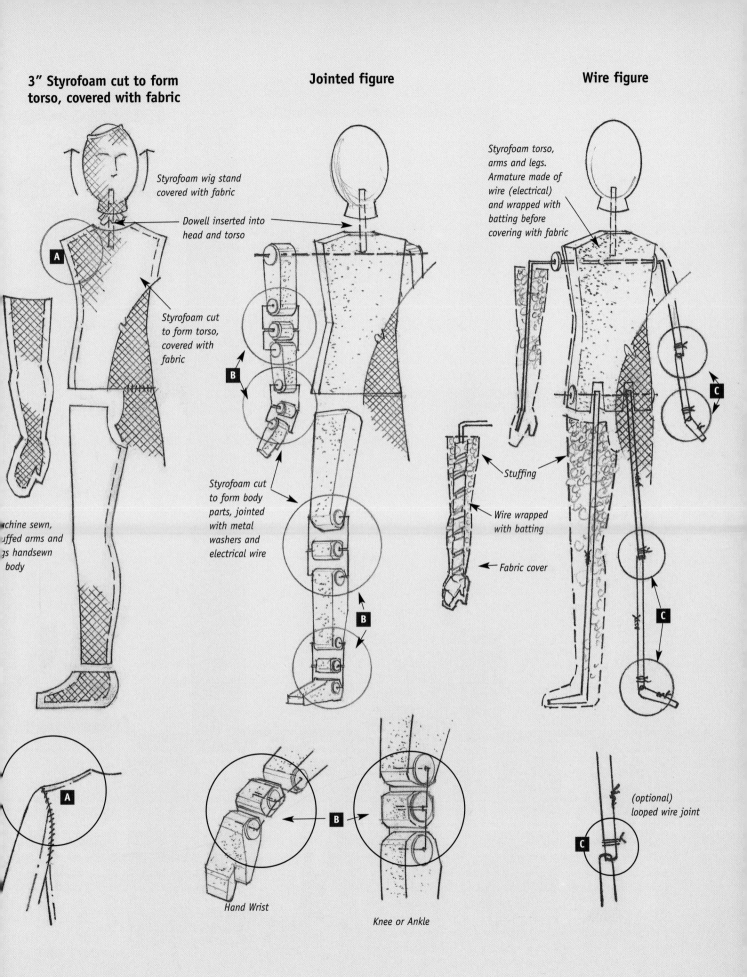

3" Styrofoam cut to form torso, covered with fabric

Jointed figure

Wire figure

Styrofoam wig stand covered with fabric

Dowell inserted into head and torso

A

Styrofoam cut to form torso, covered with fabric

B

Styrofoam torso, arms and legs. Armature made of wire (electrical) and wrapped with batting before covering with fabric

C

Stuffing

Wire wrapped with batting

Fabric cover

Styrofoam cut to form body parts, jointed with metal washers and electrical wire

B

C

...chine sewn, ...uffed arms and ...gs handsewn ...body

A

B

Hand Wrist

Knee or Ankle

C

(optional) looped wire joint

TRANSITIONS

There comes a point when no matter how much we might like to put things in tidy little boxes for book writing, they just won't go. Such is the case with the figures on these pages. What are they? Are they jointed figures? Are they armatured figures? Are they mechanical figures? Are they dolls at all? What they are is some and all of the above. The artists themselves would probably waffle a definition for these pieces. They reflect the ultimate in design: The idea and the imagineering to make the idea reality.

The important thing is that the dollmaker did not say, "On Tuesday, I will take these screws and this set of springs and make a jumping figure. I will now turn to page x in the great book of dollmaking and find the right steps." The great book of dollmaking is the world and all the possible materials and mechanical connections in it. It is more likely that the artist said, "Hmm, what would happen if I want to underline the idea of my character with a little more action? What kind of an action would bring out the emotion or character I want to express?" or "What kind of actions can I add to make the character even more expressive?" At this point, he begins to think about the problems that need solving. His imagination and what he knows or can find out about engineering results in his own very unique expression.

Emo-An Automaton by Chris Chomick and Peter Meder, 6 ½", resin, brass and steel armature, hand-made wind-up mechanisim. Construction itself can be a thing of beauty as seen in the complexities of Emo's body. Motion always adds an element of intrigue for the viewer/player. Emo rocks from side to side and gives a surprising leg kick from time to time. Photo by Chris Chomick

Roland Montague, 21", joints system, head of Cernit on posable machined brass armature. The design team of Chris Chomick and Peter Meder obviously have a definite desire to have fun with their figures. Again, the movement underlines the element of the comic and absurd that is given to the sculpted and painted expression. Roland's rather flat and stiff motion seems to emphasize his stylized movements as a "ham" actor. Notice that the design is carried out in the stiffness of Roland's rigidly styled hair-do. Photo by Chris Chomick

Cecil is certainly having a bad hair day. When a wind-up mechanism was added to give a slow back-and-forth rocking motion, the viewer can almost imagine him moaning as well. The next design step might be including a voice box. Photo by Chris Chomick

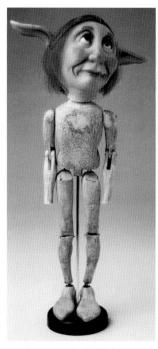

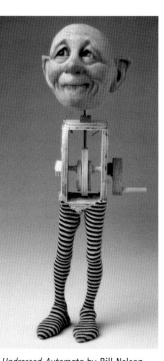

Wooden Puppet by Bill Nelson, 13". Bill Nelson's figure work started with ventriloquist's dummies. The dummy, like the puppet, is perhaps the ultimate grown-up toy. The figure's construction provides a character and a movable body—further character development is totally up to the person who acts with the figure. Photo by Bill Nelson

Undressed Automata by Bill Nelson, 17". A very simple gear action, combined with a swiveling head, will allow a figure like this to move its head up and down and from side to side. It can express positive and negative emotions, and gives motion to what would otherwise be a fixed pose. Photo by Bill Nelson

Only the Lonely by Bill Nelson, 10". From dummies, Bill Nelson moved on to making fixed-pose, wire-armatured figures, but the lure of movement for character expression was too hard to resist. The idea of loneliness expressed by the head of the figure *Only the Lonely* would have been expressed best if the figure had his head in his hands; however, if the pose had been fixed, the viewer would miss a good deal of the impact of the facial expression. Bill's problem was to come up with a way to show both the face and the head in the hands. He solved this by creating a mechanical system that moves the head and hands. Photo by Bill Nelson

Queen of Heaven and Earth by Ellen Rixford, 5' tall puppets of Celastic, foam, wood, metal and fabric. Dimensional illustrator Ellen Rixford incorporates mechanical action in many of her figures. Here, the mask movements allow four different expressions of persona that are further enhanced by interior lighting to provide eyelight and facial translucency. Photos by Ellen Rixford

UPPER LEFT: *The Mask* by Akiko Anzai, 14",
cloth with cloth over paperclay face. Photo by Akiko Anzai

UPPER RIGHT: *Phoenix* by Mary Thomas, 18", cloth.
Photo by Mary Thomas

LOWER RIGHT: *Banana Bunch* by Betsey Baker, 12", clown is La Doll
on wire armature, orangutan is Super Sculpey. Photo by Betsy Baker

UPPER LEFT: *Terra Cotta Angel* by Susan Dunham, 23", wrapped wire body with terra cotta. Photo by Susan Dunham

LOWER LEFT: *David Avalon Grows a Rose* by Maggie Mayer, needlesculpted muslin. Photo by UKA

UPPER RIGHT: *Gloriana* by Charles Batte, one-of-a-kind, 14" seated, polymer sculpture, cloth body over wire armature. Photo by Peter Marcus Photography

UPPER LEFT: *At Aunt Eleanor's Farm—After Chagall*
by Jane Darin, 25", cloth over wire armature.
Photo by Joe Darin

UPPER RIGHT: *Theresa* by Angela Talbot, 14", Fimo. Photo by Trudie Lee

LOWER RIGHT: *Babysitting* by Toyoko Matsubara, 14",
cloth needlesculpture. Photo by Junko Liesfeld

UPPER LEFT: *Old Woman in a Red Dress* by Scott R. Gray, paperclay and fabric. Photo by Roger Schreiber

LOWER LEFT: *Sun Man* by Dee Dee Triplett, 14", cloth over wire armature. Photo by Evan Bracken

UPPER RIGHT: *The Great Dame* by Robert Doucette, sculpture, and Tom Slotten, costume, 17", paperclay over wood and wire armature. Photo by Blue Trimarchi-Art Works

UPPER LEFT: *Winter Wrangler* by Judith Klawitter, 24", Super Sculpey, wire armature. Photo by Mark Bryant

UPPER RIGHT: *Attitude* by Carroll Stanley, 20", Cernit. Photo by Carroll Stanley

LOWER RIGHT: *Maggie, Tlinglit Lady* by Mary Ellen Frank, NIADA, 14", cedar head and hands, cloth body. Photo by Mary Ellen Frank

UPPER LEFT: *Kinshi Doll 1* by Jill N. Hamilton, 14",
stuffed muslin with Sculpey face. Photo by Jill N. Hamilton

LOWER LEFT: *Kinshi Doll 2* by Jill N. Hamilton, 14", stuffed muslin with
Sculpey face. Photo by Jill N. Hamilton

UPPER RIGHT: *Chocolate Delight* by June Goodnow, 14"
seated, cast resin, cloth over wire armature body. Photo by W. Don Smith

TOP: *Fable* by Jo Ellen Trilling, 13", cloth over wire armature.
Photo by Jo Ellen Trilling

LOWER RIGHT: *Talitha* by Marleen Engeler, 26" seated, porcelain.
Photo by Mark Engeler

UPPER LEFT: *Contemplation* by Marcella Welch, 18",
Cernit and cloth. Photo by Marcella Welch

LOWER LEFT: *Fantasy and Love* by Lawrence Reiter, 21",
paperclay, wood and wire armature. Photo by Lawrence
Reiter

UPPER RIGHT: *Ore-Heavy Metal Warrior-Protector of the
Queen* by Robert Cunningham, 38", Fimo over wire arma-
ture. Photo courtesy of *Contemporary Doll Collector*, Scott
Publishing, used with permission. Photo by Jan Pisarczyk,
Pirak Studios, Ltd.

UPPER LEFT: *Flying Fairy* by Dee Dee Triplett, 8", cloth over wire armature. Photo by Evan Bracken

LOWER LEFT: *Angel* by Kathryn Walmsley, 16". Cernit head and hands, cloth over wire armature body. Photo by Paul Schult

UPPER RIGHT: *Mary, Mary* by Toni Carroll, 19", paperclay. Photo by W. Don Smith

UPPER LEFT: *Summer* by Margery Cannon, 15", cloth, needlesculpted. Photo by Jan Shou

UPPER RIGHT: *Alice* by Kate Lackman, 17", fabric and paper over cast resin. Photo by Kate Lackman

Joints:
The Traditional
Approach

Everyone likes a jointed figure. They are intriguing. They are intimate and happy—you can really play with them.

When considering using joints in design, the first question to ask is: Why? Your answer should be because you want the figure to be moved or posed, you want it to be interactive with a human player, or you want to use movement to give your idea greater depth. If the full impact of the idea can be expressed as a fixed dimensional illustration, then you have no real need to make joints. Many artists choose fixed poses because they have designed for the impact to be seen in the form and sculpted details and/or costume. Playing with this type of a figure would destroy the artist's intent. They definitely do not want their pieces played with. And then there are jointed art figures made purely for mind play—to make the viewer think about movement even if it doesn't happen. When you begin to design, you will need to ask yourself what things are most important for you to show to achieve maximum impact for your piece.

There is a temptation to "play God" in figure making. We want to make a figure that as nearly as possible represents the human body. Since mechanics always impress the

Barnacle Belle by Jane Darin, 13", jointed cloth. Photo by Joe Darin

viewer, we tend to think that the best figure will have jointed movement. Not so. Figure makers are artists and the business of art is suggestion. We want a viewer to think about or react to the piece. We want him to fill in the blanks from his own reactions and experience. The ideal jointed figure would be able to mimic the human body and, like the human structure, the workings would be invisibly embedded below the surface. With the animatronic knowledge and bionics available, we could probably create very human-like figures, but they would be "tell all" figures with very little left for the viewer to have fun with mentally or emotionally.

Before you go bulleting off into joint creations, don't forget to go back and look at your original idea or concept. Your initial design concept should have given you a pretty good idea of what the overall aesthetic look of the piece will be, or what you want it to look like. In some happy cases, the initial concept might have appeared with a jointing application or as the result of your knowledge of jointing. A wood carver or a fabric figure maker might always think of a jointed concept whereas clay sculptors may not. The type of finished material also dictates, but should not stop, the type of joints that can be used. If you want motion, it can be achieved—you just have to figure out the type of joint that will work best with your material.

The idea of making a movable sculpture is not new. Jointed figures were found in graves or tombs that date back several thousand years. The doll figure became a popular novelty for fashion and for adult amusement in the 1600s—at the same time as watch making and other mechanical applications—so it is not surprising that most of the basic joint ideas for dolls had been explored and developed before the end of the nineteenth century. Indeed, with the exception of animatronics, most of the techniques we use today have been available for two hundred to two thousand years. The only differences are in what individual artists have added or changed to create something unique in their own work.

Augustine's Augmentation, May West, Teatime for the Soul by Lizzie Oz Primozic, 26", 31", 26", fabric collage, flowers, buttons, beads, collage image transfer. Photo by Tim Safranek Photographics

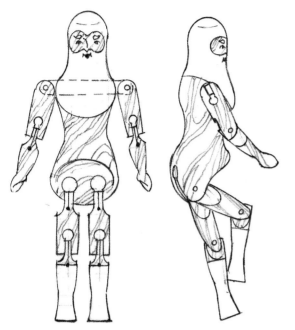

Doll manufacturers in the nineteenth century invented a number of interesting variations. This drawing of an antique doll shows the typical mortise and tenon joint where one limb is captured by a forked piece in the end of the other. Note how the crosspiece in the torso effectively stops extreme motion of the leg, and how the placement of the shoulder joint on a rotating dowel allows more than one arm movement. The box-like torso was meant to contain a voice box. Study antique dolls to see what other variations can be done with joints.

Rotating dowell

Crosspiece stops leg action

Wooden joints like those sketched from a figure in the author's collection made by Dick Showalter were probably adapted from carpentry, used for ceramic forms and carved wooden figures, and redesigned for cloth. Note that it is the designer's choice as to which end of the limb is the receiver and which the extension.

Spirit's Rhapsody by Lorri Acott Fowler, 27", stoneware. Photo by Lorri Acott Fowler

Grounded by Lorri Acott Fowler, 22", stoneware. Photo by Lorri Acott Fowler

Sleeping Princess by Susanna Oroyan, 18", air-drying stone clay. Photo by W. Don Smith

COMMON OR TYPICAL JOINTS

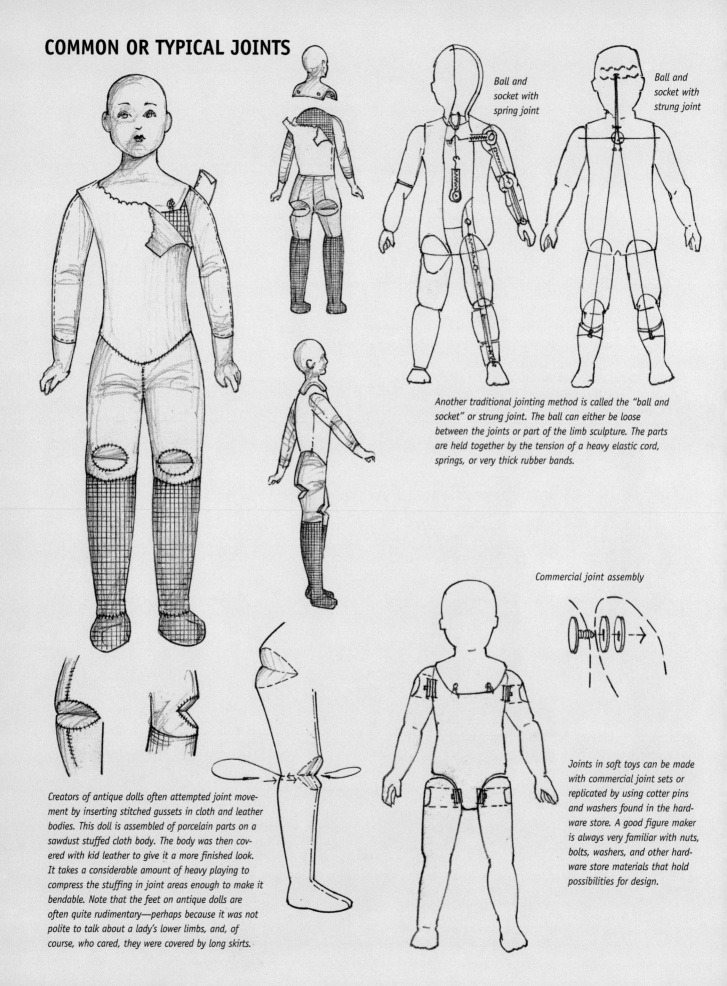

Ball and socket with spring joint

Ball and socket with strung joint

Another traditional jointing method is called the "ball and socket" or strung joint. The ball can either be loose between the joints or part of the limb sculpture. The parts are held together by the tension of a heavy elastic cord, springs, or very thick rubber bands.

Commercial joint assembly

Joints in soft toys can be made with commercial joint sets or replicated by using cotter pins and washers found in the hardware store. A good figure maker is always very familiar with nuts, bolts, washers, and other hardware store materials that hold possibilities for design.

Creators of antique dolls often attempted joint movement by inserting stitched gussets in cloth and leather bodies. This doll is assembled of porcelain parts on a sawdust stuffed cloth body. The body was then covered with kid leather to give it a more finished look. It takes a considerable amount of heavy playing to compress the stuffing in joint areas enough to make it bendable. Note that the feet on antique dolls are often quite rudimentary—perhaps because it was not polite to talk about a lady's lower limbs, and, of course, who cared, they were covered by long skirts.

JOINT PHYSICS

In the human body, muscles and tendons are attached to the bones throughout their length—not just at the joint site. The joint does not move itself. It is moved by push-pull muscle and tendon action at different locations, and each of these actions has a different degree of strength. In a simple button or gusset doll joint, the joint itself allows the movement, but it has no muscle tendon action to stop or hold position against gravity.

When we want a figure to stand up and/or hold position, we can achieve the joint action (bending) and the muscle and tendon action (strength) with wire. If we want the figure to be movable, we need to incorporate the joint. If we want it to be movable and fixable, then we have to add things like weights and springs to stop the action at the desired point. And when we re-create the human bone structure in the joint, we need to "end-stop" it so the bone itself will stop rotation. This is where creative imagineering can get exciting.

When we translate vectors or lines of muscle and tendon force into dollmaking terms, we are forced to simplify human structure. Additionally, depending on materials, we cannot exert the amount of force necessary to counteract gravity.

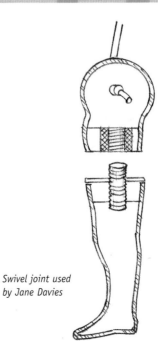

Down? by Jane Davies, 6", cast porcelain, nine joints. Photo by Jane Davies

Fleur (body and finished figure) by Lynn and Michael Roche, 17", porcelain. Photo by Michael and Lynne Roche

Swivel joint used by Jane Davies

JOINTS IN THEORY AND SIMPLE PRACTICE

The human joint is a wonderful apparatus. Its basic function is to allow us to stand up, move ourselves, and manipulate things in our environment. Its marvelous engineering efficiency allows just enough directed motion to perform a set of functions with maximum efficiency. For instance, the hip allows the whole leg to move backward and forward with some degree of rotation, and the knee streamlines this motion by making a very limited rotation and directed motion up and down to the back only. The same is true of the arm—gross movement at the shoulder, more directed movement at the elbow, many refined movements at the wrists and fingers.

When you begin to design a joint for a figure, you need to remember that the human joint is directed and aided by the muscles and tendons, which you might not have in your figure construction. If you do not choose to use a strung joint (simulating muscles and tendons), your joint formation will have to convey all the motions itself. And the joint action needs to be both directed and stopped—something will have to simulate a knee cap and keep the lower leg from making a 180 degree arc, something will have to minimize wrist and ankle side-to-side motion.

Many craftsmen have been tempted by clothespins—they look so much like a human figure we can't resist bringing them to life with joints. The pinned pin or clothespin doll joint was my first hands-on experience with joints, and it is a good way to understand the principle of the pinned or pegged joint.

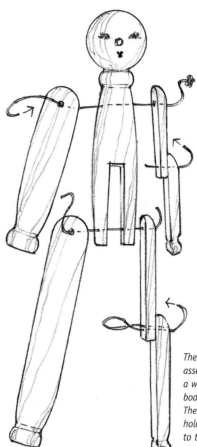

The parts are assembled by running a wire through the body and limbs. The wire is bent to hold the limb close to the body.

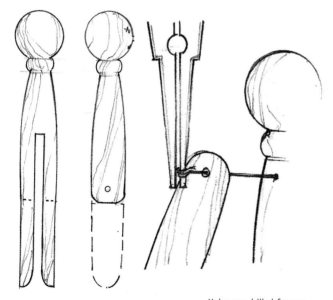

Clothespin with a bead glued on top for a head. Legs are separated by sawing off pin ends.

Holes are drilled for arm and leg attachment.

Joe College and the Pretty Pink Lady by Susanna Oroyan, 15" wood. We always want to see what happens if we do a bit more. Still using no more than a darning needle, a big wooden bead, a piece of 1x2" fir, a small saw, a wood rasp, and household hardware, I put together two figures with a marionette type of joint. Photo by W. Don Smith.

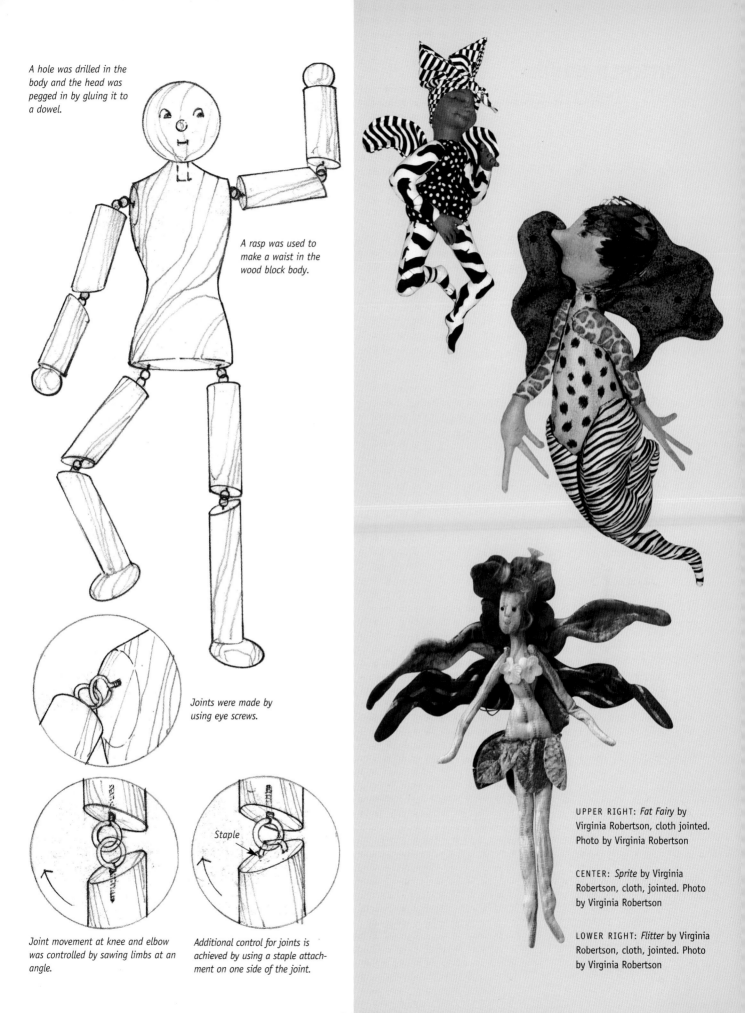

A hole was drilled in the body and the head was pegged in by gluing it to a dowel.

A rasp was used to make a waist in the wood block body.

Joints were made by using eye screws.

Joint movement at knee and elbow was controlled by sawing limbs at an angle.

Additional control for joints is achieved by using a staple attachment on one side of the joint.

Staple

UPPER RIGHT: *Fat Fairy* by Virginia Robertson, cloth jointed. Photo by Virginia Robertson

CENTER: *Sprite* by Virginia Robertson, cloth, jointed. Photo by Virginia Robertson

LOWER RIGHT: *Flitter* by Virginia Robertson, cloth, jointed. Photo by Virginia Robertson

STITCHED JOINTS

A dollmaker will try any method with any material. By far the most difficult type of a joint is one made with a soft, stuffed body. Because the resilient stuffing tends to move around, it's very difficult to maintain the straight vector needed for correct movement. In short, stuffed cloth has very little resistance. When attaching parts through the body, there is simply nothing to pull against. For this reason, cloth dolls achieve jointing by exterior attachments—the button and the gusseted/or sling joint are most commonly used for cloth dolls.

Untitled by Pamela Cowart Rickman, NIADA, 14", cloth, gesso, colored pencils, acrylics. Photo by Richard Dorbin

Single stitching attaches parts, but is a little too uncontrolled to satisfactorily mimic human motion.

Placement of the stitches limits arm to backward and forward motion.

Placement of the stitches allows motion to be directed at the hip, but the lower leg could over-rotate.

Stitching through the body at the shoulder can restrain arm motion.

Designing the cloth body to include a hip/pelvis can help to control motion.

ELINOR'S JOINTS

A dollmaker will find ways to get desired effects. elinor peace bailey studied older doll forms and successfully adopted joint forms from wood and cloth traditions to achieve a very pleasing movement in her cloth dolls.

Send in that Clown by elinor peace bailey, jointed cloth. Photo by Isaac Bailey

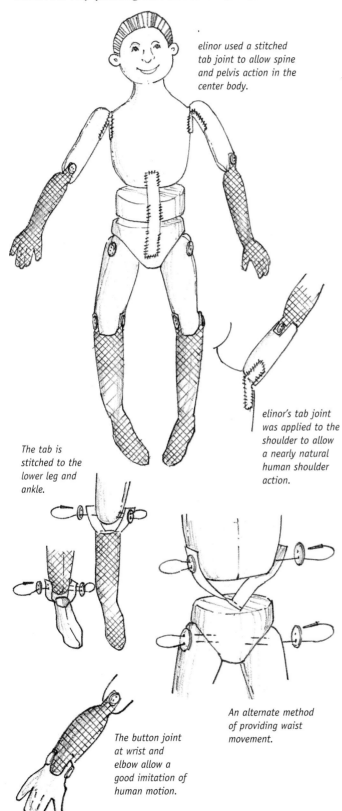

elinor used a stitched tab joint to allow spine and pelvis action in the center body.

elinor's tab joint was applied to the shoulder to allow a nearly natural human shoulder action.

The tab is stitched to the lower leg and ankle.

An alternate method of providing waist movement.

The button joint at wrist and elbow allow a good imitation of human motion.

Sophie and Abe (above and below) by elinor peace bailey, 13", jointed cloth. Photos by Isaac Bailey

HEAD ATTACHMENTS

Here are some methods of attaching heads that can be applied to soft figures.

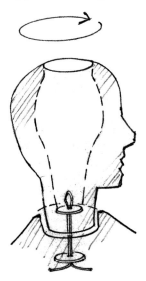

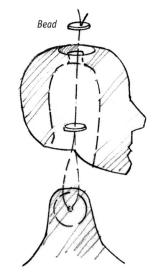

A joint made with a washer and cotter pin is inserted to connect the head and body before stuffing parts.

A bead is inserted into a neck stub and the head is attached by stitching through the bead to the top of the head. Stitches at top can be made more secure by sewing through a bead.

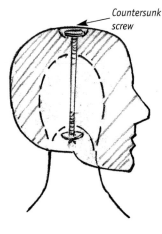

Countersunk screw

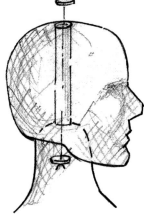

A solid spacer made of metal tubing can keep a stuffed head from collapsing.

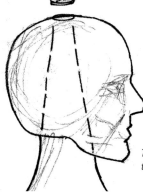

The neck stub can be extended through the stuffed head.

THE HIDDEN CLOTH JOINT

The phrase "can't be done" does not exist in the doll-maker vocabulary. After experimenting with the typical cloth joints, I decided that I wanted to improve on them by attempting a neater look with a ball and socket action. I had no difficulty in creating wrist, ankle, knee, and elbow joints that worked quite nicely and had a smooth look.

When it came to doing the ball and socket for shoulder and hip, I had to pause and think about additional internal support if those joints were to move by stringing tension. The first solution was to give up the idea, the second was to make a very hard stuffed body and a joint set arrangement. The third solution required what we can call a spacer. And in designing the spacer, at least three different possibilities were considered.

The solution used wooden beads as shown.

VISIBLE BEAD SPACER

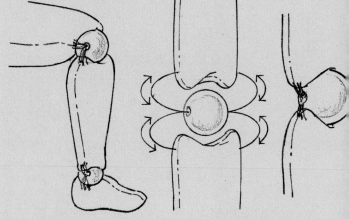

A wooden bead is placed between two stuffed limbs and attached by hand stitching.

The bead is placed inside the lower leg piece at knee.

BURIED BEAD JOINT

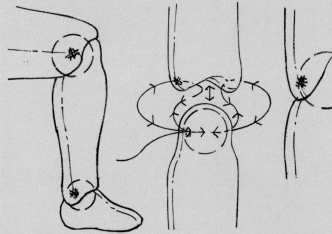

Fabric from the upper leg is pulled down and stitched from the outside of the upper leg through the bead in the lower leg.

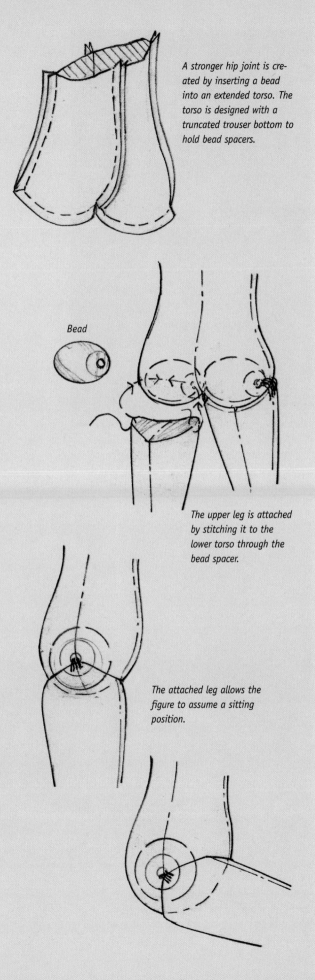

A stronger hip joint is created by inserting a bead into an extended torso. The torso is designed with a truncated trouser bottom to hold bead spacers.

Bead

The upper leg is attached by stitching it to the lower torso through the bead spacer.

The attached leg allows the figure to assume a sitting position.

BURIED JOINTS

The dollmaker who wants to realistically represent both the look and the action of the human body often wants to hide the joints. A fine example of the buried joint is the one developed for the posable fashion figure. Here, hard plastic "bones" are joined and the resulting skeleton is covered over with a soft vinyl skin.

The home-studio dollmaker can approach a solution for a buried joint by sculpting the figure in a hard material and then covering it with a soft, stretchy fabric such as Lycra, leather, velour, or hosiery fabric.

Other examples of the buried joint have been developed by George Stuart and Lisa Lichtenfels, who essentially create a jointed wire armature. Both artists do this in order to achieve a very realistic look, although the action is only applied by the artist to achieve a final life-like pose. Neither intend the viewer to play with their figures. Many of Stuart's figures have been made for museum displays, and the jointing action he created allows him to reassemble figures if he wishes to change character.

Some forms of film animation use a buried armature. Here a posable joint is covered with material (usually vinyl) that gives the outward sculptural form. The figure is posed, the film is shot, and the animator opens the joint, reposes it, and film is shot for the next piece of the action. More recent advances have allowed the animator to electronically move the figure without having to use a screwdriver to adjust the joints. Compared to the capabilities of virtual reality/computer-generated animation where human actors suit up electronically and computers record their actions and overlay graphics, it may be that actual mechanical or even electronic animation will become a thing of the past. However, dimensional illustrators and puppeteers should find some food for thought in these applications.

Kriemhild's Revenge by George Stuart, $1/4$ life-size, mixed media, articulated skeleton, fixed poses, fabric woven to order. Photo by Peter d'Aprix

JOINT MATERIAL CONSIDERATIONS

It follows from the discussion of joint physics that the easiest kind of joint to make is one of hard material. The harder, more resistant the material, the better we can direct the vectors. Traditionally, the best hard joints have been made of wood, kiln-fired clay, or contemporary plastics and compositions.

Polymer clays (Fimo®, Cernit , or Sculpey) and paper-clays can be used to make jointed figures. These materials are not quite as hard, and when used for small, thin parts, can break under joint stringing tension. If parts are painted, there could also be some deterioration from wear. Joints with these materials can and have been done, but the doing of them requires thought and care.

The closest a dollmaker can get to simulating human action is through the use of a spring-loaded/counter-weighted joint and/or the simulation of muscle action by counter-placed elastic stringing or springs.

Jordan Marsh by Elizabeth Brandon, 16", all porcelain, 17 joints, costume by Virginia Studyvin. Photo by David L. Cobb

Jessie, one of the four figures from *The Journey* by Martha Armstrong-Hand. Photo by Larry Barbier

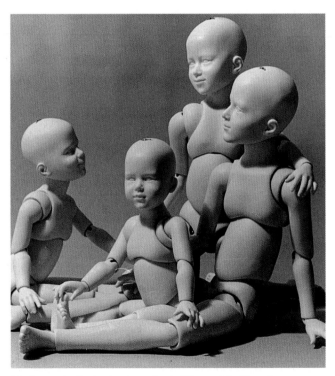

The Journey by Martha Armstrong-Hand, 18", porcelain. These figures were made to depict the artist's daughters about to make a very important journey in 1958. Dressed, they wear coats and dresses and carry luggage typical of that year. Their complex joints allow them to be posed in any number of life-like positions. Note the additional joint piece at the shoulder that allows the arm to move across the torso back or front. (See stringing diagram) Photo by Larry Barbier

Head attachment and knee joint design by Elizabeth Brandon

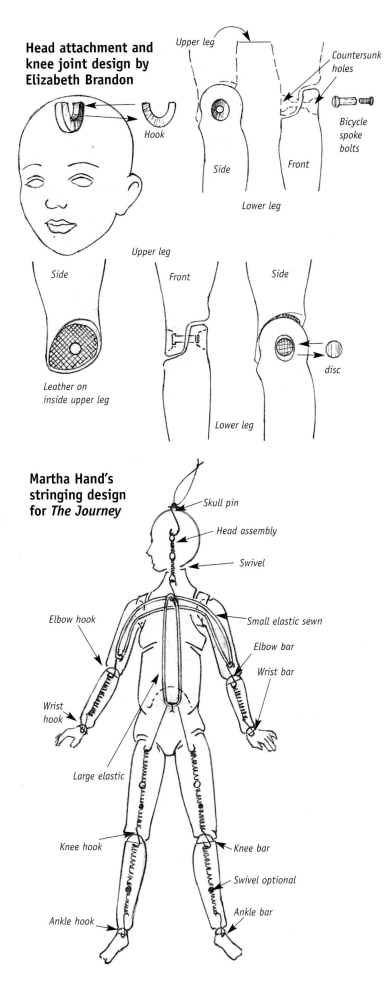

Upper leg

Countersunk holes

Hook

Side

Front

Bicycle spoke bolts

Lower leg

Side

Upper leg

Front

Side

Leather on inside upper leg

disc

Lower leg

Martha Hand's stringing design for *The Journey*

Skull pin

Head assembly

Swivel

Elbow hook

Small elastic sewn

Elbow bar

Wrist bar

Wrist hook

Large elastic

Knee hook

Knee bar

Swivel optional

Ankle bar

Ankle hook

Merle Tennent by Elizabeth Brandon, 16", porcelain, 13 joints, costume by Virginia Studyvin. Photo by David L. Cobb

■ Artists Elizabeth Brandon, Martha Armstrong-Hand, and Jane Davies (see page 109) have worked to perfect the jointing of porcelain figures. Their work is time consuming and exacting, but ultimately a rewarding experience and a delight to behold. It is also indicative of design as an on-going process throughout the creation of a piece.

Artists who work with cast porcelain typically begin by sculpting a full figure of oil-based clay (plasticine) on a working armature. When the form of the figure is satisfactory, it is cut apart and taken off the working armature support. A mold is made and the figure is cast in wax. The mold allows several casts to be made if experimentation with joint cuts or mold part lines is necessary. The wax castings are also tooled to arrive at a final, very smooth finish necessary to release from the porcelain casting mold. When the wax model parts are satisfactory, the artist then makes a final mold or set of molds that are used to cast the porcelain. For jointed parts with more than one opening, considerable thought must be given to the mold construction itself. When the parts are fired, painted, and ready to assemble, the artists apply their own versions of the ball and socket or strung joint. The full figure drawing shows the basic assembly method used by Martha Armstrong Hand. Both Jane and Elizabeth use similar methods with variations in the details.

JOINT DESIGN

Most of us tend to think of wood in connection with jointed figures. The work of Floyd Bell and Ken Von Essen is proof that not many doll designers go neatly into set boxes—not even the people who do it.

Although the art of kiln-fired clay has been known to man for millennia, it did not become a figure-making medium until the eighteenth century. Wood, however, was available almost everywhere. It could be shaped with any kind of knife, and it had the added advantage of being fairly durable. Moreover, when carved and smoothed, the grain and surface made it look and feel good.

Dollmakers have had centuries to perfect the art of hand-carving figures. The work of Bell and Von Essen show both the beauty and the excitement of the handmade jointed wood figure.

Typically a wood figure begins with a sketch and a pattern drawing. Most artists will enlarge the drawing to the desired finished size and trace the parts onto the wood. The wood form is then sawed out into the rough shapes. Knives and chisels are used to refine the parts. As the figure nears its final form, the artist works to integrate joint mechanisms with the finished carving. When the mechanics are in place, final fine carving and finishing are done to make each jointed area well-blended and smooth as well as functional.

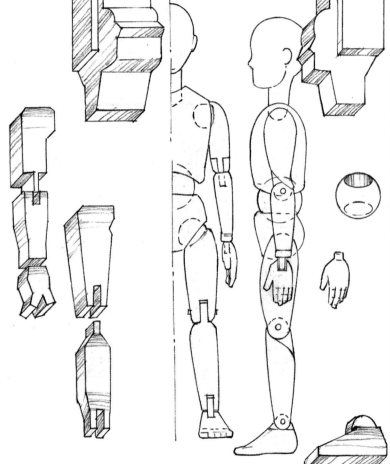

Parts for a figure being made by Floyd Bell are transferred from the original drawing to the wood and sawn out. This figure will be jointed with ball and socket and friction joints. Note how the elbow and knee are designed to allow control of the direction of motion. Bell began making figures as a challenge to and method of inspiring his wood-shop students. As a result, his high school students have been able to undertake commissioned work, and a scholarship fund has been established.

Josephine Baker by Floyd Bell, hand carved wood.
Photo by W. Don Smith

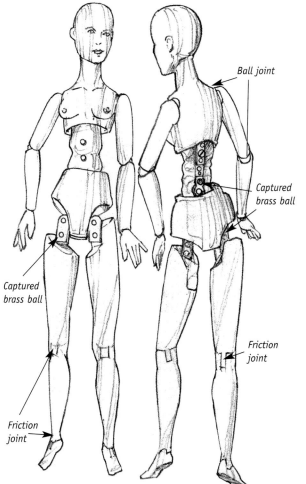

Ball joint

Captured
brass ball

Captured
brass ball

Friction
joint

Friction
joint

Front and back view of a figure made by Ken Von Essen.
Ken's figure will use a combination of ball, friction, and
captured joints. Note the use of a double captured joint
to effect waist movement.

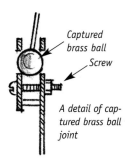

Captured
brass ball

Screw

A detail of cap-
tured brass ball
joint

Slot

Disc

Detail of friction joint.
Disc attaches to leg
and fits into slot

Peddler, detail of waist and
hip joint. Photo by Ken Von
Essen

Peddler by Ken Von Essen, 24", hand-carved black
walnut. Photo by Ken Von Essen

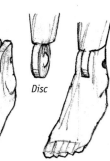

Ballerina by Ken Von Essen,
26", hand-carved and jointed
wood. Photo by Ken Von Essen

Ruby by Ken Von Essen, 28",
hand-carved black walnut.
Photo by Ken Von Essen

Cloth Figures

DESIGN CONSIDERATIONS

Anyone who has ever sewn two pieces of cloth together and stuffed the resulting shape learned that cloth is a very sculptable material. The pliable weave or stretch of the fabric gives cloth a wonderful modeling potential. It can be filled or pulled over a form, cut and assembled three-dimensionally by sewing (or gluing), and stitched into a permanent position. Cloth will do just about everything a hard sculpting material can do. It will just look different in a greater variety of ways.

The first cloth consideration is that it does not have to be stuffed. Most of us know that making a stuffed figure well can be just as demanding and difficult as sculpting. Almost every type of dollmaking involves cloth, but wonderful effects can be achieved by wrapping, stretching, and surface stitching without having to fill it. Try some.

The second cloth consideration is that it does not have to be plain-weave cotton. Most cloth dollmakers begin with a background in home sewing—either dressmaking or quilting. They also often begin by using purchased patterns. The common denominator for these is plain woven cotton fabric. It is easy to cut, sew, and stuff. It comes in an amazing array of patterns and colors. Calico, however, is not the beginning and end material. It is simply one design consideration among many. Unfortunately, calico is not always used to its best advantage in doll design. Poor design with calico occurs when a maker uses a complex technique for body or face construction and finishes the piece with calico prints and costume cuts that do not match in color intensity or scale. Always consider the best combinations of fabrics. Think a minute: The felt dolls originated by Madame Lenci in the 1920s and still produced today are cloth, but they have felt bodies and costumes of felt juxtaposed with stiff, light organdy. Some very effective dolls have been made in suedecloth and Ultrasuede® flat goods and these look well juxtaposed with knits.

The third cloth consideration is that it does not have to be cloth. Time and time again, I find that an initial idea that I had for a cloth figure will not achieve the effect I want in cloth. I have to re-think the materials used for the idea. This is going to happen with any medium. Designing is the picking and choosing of things that will work for the idea.

Mother-in-Law by Lynne A. Calhoun and Debbi McCullough, 14", cloth, free-standing. Photo by Lynne Calhoun

Rosie Ram by Andrea L. Stern, 22", cloth, bead-loom work face. Photo by Andrea L. Stern

Shirley by Diana S. Baumbauer, 22", cotton knit soft sculpture. Photo by Diana S. Baumbauer

Come With Me, Lucille by Dru Esslinger, 12", cloth. Photo by Les Bricker

Bayou Bebe by Amy Wickstrom, 30", felt and cloth. Photo by Mark Simar

Alfreda Mulroni by Penny Mason, 18", cloth, needlesculpted face, armatured limbs. Photo by Penny Mason

Gladwin the Aborigine Girl by Hedy Katin, 15", molded cloth face, cloth body. Photo by Hedy Katin

DIMENSION AND DEPTH: THE PUCKERLESS PIECE

When we sew two flat pieces of fabric together and stuff them, we can get frustrated because the stuffing creates a distortion or warping in the cloth and the seams pucker. Even if you cut the flat piece with a curved edge, you still have pucker problems. The problem is that we are trying to make flat things (fabric) go over round things (stuffing). So, the question is, How do you get from flat to round? The fabric figure designer uses dressmaker's tricks: contours, gussets, gathers, and darts.

The following pages show how a flat pattern for a "pancake" shaped doll can be adjusted to become a fully dimensional piece by the insertion of darts. The steps will lead anyone who tries them to a fairly realistic representation of a human female figure. Further experimentation with outline and dart shapes will bring the designer to more original and unique forms, and to forms that might solve a particular desire—such as a tall, skinny, flat-chested type or a short, chubby type with broad hips.

The Wreathmaker by Delores Cumming, 18", cloth over paper-clay face, velour body. Photo by Delores Cumming

Messenger 1 & Messenger 2 by Susanna Oroyan, 22", cloth over wire armature. This figure was developed using the process shown for developing a dimensional pattern with the dressmaker dart. Photo by W. Don Smith

Rollo by Sandra L. Feingold, 18", paper and cloth. Photo by Sandra L. Feingold

The Blue and Orange Abstractions by Susanna Oroyan, 12" and 15", stuffed felt. The perfectly flat figure can be a starting point for developing a fully dimensional figure. Photo by W. Don Smith

Dolores by Lorna Easter, muslin. Photo by Robert Hirsch

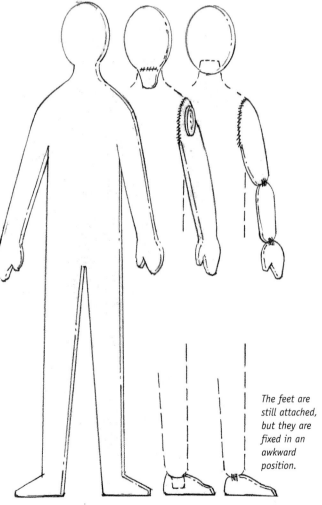

Gray Goolie by Susanna Oroyan, 18", gathered and stuffed knit. Photo by Susanna Oroyan

The feet are still attached, but they are fixed in an awkward position.

Start with a two-piece body pattern. Remove the arms, feet, and head. Make some decisions about the final shaping of those parts (or adjust curves to fit your design sketch).

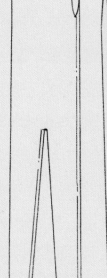

This is how the two-piece pattern would look when sewn...very flat. The remaining shape has no defined depth. If you sew and stuff a flat two-piece pattern that looks like this, the result is a uniform expansion. The figure has no back and front and its depth has no relation to the human body.

To add more depth, you would separate the pattern into four pieces. Now there are two pieces for the front and two for the back If you delete fabric in the lower back by making a curve it will create a more natural crotch and width at the buttocks. The deeper you make this curve, the larger the area will be. However, in order to compensate for the deletion, you will need to add to the body on the side at the hip.

A *To define a waist, a dart is drawn onto the front pattern pieces. Front darts have maximum width at the waist and extend equally above and below the waist on a female figure. On a male figure, the darts will be more narrow and extended.*

B *To define the lower back and give more rounding to the upper buttocks, a dart is placed in each back piece. In order to control the curve of the back, notice the widest part of the dart falls at the waist, and the dart is made longer and narrower above the waist.*

C *To further shape buttocks/hip, a dart may be placed in the side at the hip line. To compensate, an amount equal to one-half of the dart must be added at the shoulder. A tucked or dead-end dart can be made below the buttocks. When sewing, it is best to leave an opening extending above and below the back waist. When hand-sewing to close after stuffing, stitches can be placed to accentuate the lower back curve.*

D *To add bust depth, a dart is placed in the upper side of the front at the desired bust line. As any dart takes up and shortens fabric, the pattern must be lengthened/raised at the shoulder half the width of the dart.*

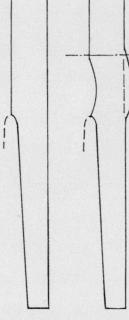

Butterfly Lady by Jacqueline Casey, 16", needle-modeled muslin. Photo by Jacqueline Casey

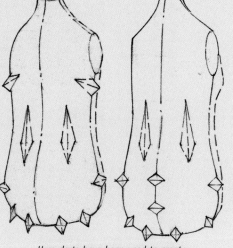
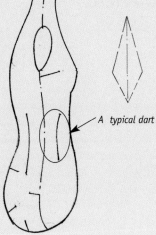
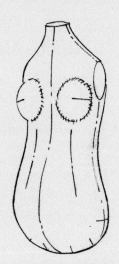

Darts are created by folding the fabric and sewing to take a tuck. Note that the dart extends beyond the outline shape on the edges so the basic outline will be maintained.

Here darts have been used to create a highly contoured female figure.

The body now has a basic female shape.

A typical dart

Additional bust shaping may be added by appliqué.

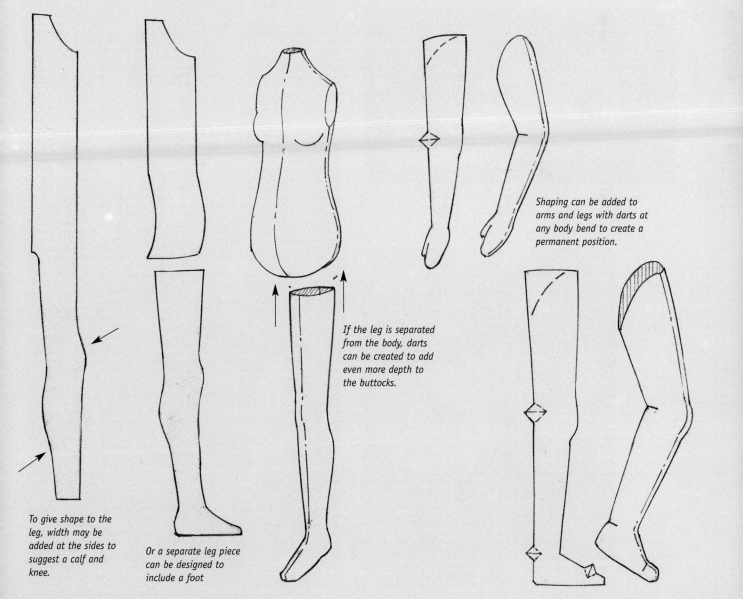

To give shape to the leg, width may be added at the sides to suggest a calf and knee.

Or a separate leg piece can be designed to include a foot

If the leg is separated from the body, darts can be created to add even more depth to the buttocks.

Shaping can be added to arms and legs with darts at any body bend to create a permanent position.

DESIGN DEVELOPMENT: GATHERS AND BAGS

Often a word will give you a starting point to develop an idea—or pull you out of a dead end. "Joint", "gather," "dart," "bigger," "smaller," "separated," "rotated," etc., can inspire explorations in entirely new directions. For instance, gathers will reduce volume to fit a particular space. Hand sewing gathered pieces to a basic body can be a quick way of creating volume. Language and talking to yourself using directional words is a major part of design work.

On the opposite page are three design developments for a basic body achieved by applying the words "separate" and "darts/gathers" to the bust and "heavier" to the body. On one hand, the result is three different versions of the bust, and, perhaps, a separate corset. On the other, the problem of making a seated figure look like it is really held in place by the force of gravity is achieved by thinking "heavier" and creating a weight bag.

The Bridge Club Ladies by Susanna Oroyan, 15", felt and needlesculpture. Photo by W. Don Smith

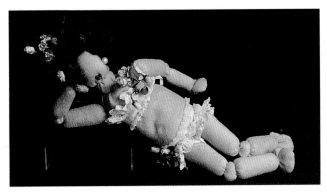

Pink Puff-a-Love by Susanna Oroyan, 15", stuffed and gathered velour. This figure and its clothing were developed by using gathers as the design feature. Photo by W. Don Smith

Hansel and Gretel by Kathi Clarke, 6", cloth needlesculpted face, cloth body over wire armature. Photo by Kathi Clarke

Ramina by Gerda Rasmussen, 28", cloth. Photo by Jorgen G. Rasmussen

BUST OVERLAY WITH GATHERS

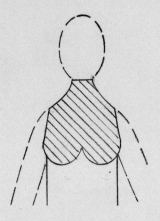

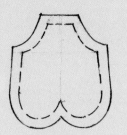

Bust pattern cut along basic pattern shoulder line and extended slightly at each side.

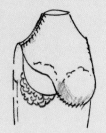

Bust pattern fabric hand-sewn at shoulders and neck, stuffing inserted.

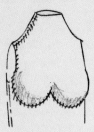

Bust bottom-gathered and hand-stitched to body.

BUST GATHERED CORSET STYLE

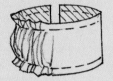

Straight piece of fabric gathered to form bust or costume top.

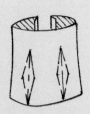

Darts sewn into pieces cut to fit body.

A sewn corset bottom.

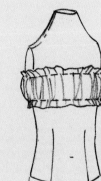

The two pieces sewn together to make a corset or gathered bodice.

MAKING A WEIGHT BAG FOR A SEATED DOLL

D   D

Cut 2

C   C
B   B
A   A

Pattern shape for a weight bag.

Leave open

D
D
B
B   A   A
C

To form box pleats, match A to C on each side, and sew from B to AC (on both pieces, 2 pleats per piece). Put pieces right sides together and sew from D to D around the shape. Leave top open for filling.

A weight bag placed inside a figure.

The bottom of the bag becomes the bottom of the doll's torso.

Side view of completed figure.

DESIGN DEVELOPMENT: HEADS

The head construction on the opposite page shows how designers modify their own patterns or get inspirations from others. Several years ago, a chance remark by designer Virginia Robertson led to my design of *Modella* to allow width in a head by using a chin gusset and a curved seam at the forehead. The head on the opposite page shows a refinement of that concept as developed by Virginia Robertson. Virginia's version allows for a more defined nose and more realistic head shape, which she wanted as a base for doing a needlesculpted, painted face. When I saw Virginia's curved version, I immediately thought of extending the chin gusset piece and head back pieces to make one complete upper torso, and that's how design evolves.

Many dollmakers need to be inventors because what they know they need to make an idea reality does not exist in the real world. Achieving satisfactory eyes for a piece is a case in point. Here, artists have had to make their own eyes because commercial glass eyes in the sizes needed are usually not as detailed or consistent in pairing as the artist wants. For years, I got around the eye problem by simply painting them; however, variety is the spice of the doll world and I did borrow some techniques from polymer artists to make my own. I used a mixture of white and transparent Fimo for the whites of the eyes, and a variety of polymer clay colors and a caning technique to make the iris. Additional natural effects can be had by using colored pens or pencils to suggest blood vessels and clear gloss sealers to make a shine. The drawings on the opposite page show how these can be set into a cloth-over-clay mask face.

Face masks in progress by Susanna Oroyan. Photo by W. Don Smith

Selection of cloth-over-clay face masks by Susanna Oroyan. Photo by W. Don Smith

Nude Nancy by Viriginia Robertson. Photo by Virginia Robertson

SUSANNA OROYAN:
"Modella" head with chin gusset

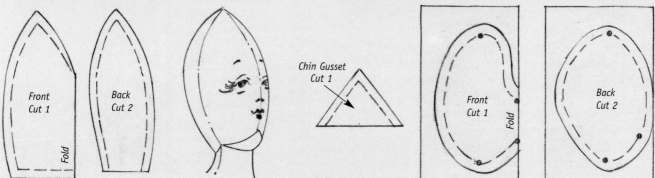

VIRGINIA ROBERTSON:
Pattern refinement with curved head and nose extension

Virginia Robertson's pattern sewn, covered, and ready for needlesculpted features

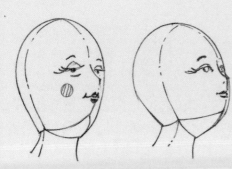

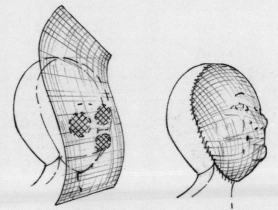

Face padded with stuffing and covered with fabric.
Face covering needlesculpted to show features.

SETTING EYES IN A CLOTH-COVERED MASK FACE

A sculpted clay mask with eye socket cut-out.

The sculpted mask covered with cloth and cut at eye socket.

The fabric is pushed into the eye socket.

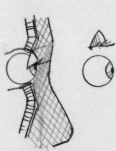

The eye is placed in the socket.

Mask with eye in socket.

A piece of fabric is glued over the eyeball to create an eyelid.

DIMENSION WITH CONTOUR

The easiest way to understand dimension by contour is to think in terms of a spacer—a third piece that is put between a back and a front so the stuffing can be comfortably accommodated. If the spacer has a straight edge, then all you will acheive is depth. If the spacer has a curved edge, you get both depth and a change in the outline of the form. When the spacer runs uniformly around an entire pattern piece, we call that a contoured shape.

You can control areas of depth by adding gussets between two flat pattern pieces. In dressmaking a gusset is usually a squarish shape added under the arm when the sleeve is of one piece with the body. The gusset allows the fabric to go around the arm but still maintain its flat pattern appearance. It might help in your design work to think of an orange as a round ball shape made by sewing together a number of gussets.

Spirit of Christmas Past by Nancy J. Laverick, 15", cloth. Nancy makes use of contours to give depth to patterns developed from fabric scrap shapes. Photo by Nancy Laverick

My Dolls by Susanna Oroyan, 14", cloth. This figure has a two-piece, bell-shaped body, extended at the hip by insertion of a fabric-covered cardboard gusset. Photo by W. Don Smith

Old Bats in Hats by Susanna Oroyan, 9", stuffed cloth. Note the hats on these figures were made by felting dryer lint with fabric stiffener. Photo by W. Don Smith

Woman on the Edge of Time by Pamela Hastings, 12", Ultrasuede. Photo by Allen Bryan

Head

Girl Sleeve

Boy Sleeve

Sleeve Gusset

Hand

Boy Pant Leg or
enlarge for Girl Skirt

Boy Side
Gusset

Leg Gusset

Center
Body

Foot

These shapes show how pattern pieces may be
developed from interesting curves and outlines
by inserting gussets. The location of dimensional
depth can be decided by the designer. Notice how
a gusset at the top of the sleeve can give a
puffed sleeve cap look, but when placed at the
bottom, the sleeve becomes a bell shape.
A contoured spacer provides uniform depth in
the upper torso, and by changing the point of
attachment for the torso, a bust or a bloused
look can be achieved. The girl's skirt is a wider
version of one trouser leg pattern.

The Sailor and His Girl by Susanna Oroyan, 15", stuffed
felt. Photo by W. Don Smith

MULTIPLE PERSONALITIES: THE INTERCHANGEABLE HEAD

There is nothing new under the sun. Almost all designs are variations on something that has been done before—sometimes in a different medium or for an entirely different use. Look, learn, and adapt for yourself. Here is one that intrigued me. In kiln-fired ceramics, heads are commonly made in one piece with a chest and upper back. This is usually referred to as a breastplate doll. What if we translated this concept to cloth?

Wouldn't it be fun to have a boxful of heads with different hair-dos, expressions, and headgear to play with? In design the important thing is what you can do with what you have. New design developments happen when we question things we have: Why does the breastplate have to be a hard material? What happens if we make it from cloth?

When I asked myself that question, I got several answers including one shown on the opposite page. In this version, the four-piece stuffed head is attached to the neck and upper chest pieces. The neck/chest pieces are cut smaller than the full torso and lined, which results in a hollow neck much like a finger puppet. I could make a body and allow it to have an assortment of heads to be attached according to the mood of the doll or my whim. One little new twist goes a long way, too. Why not make interchangeable body parts? What would you use to make the attachments? Snaps, hooks, Velcro®? See what you could do with this idea.

Group of Figaro Figures by Jill N. Hamilton. Photo by Jill Hamilton

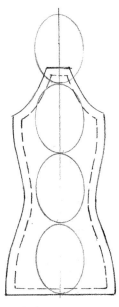

Basic torso pattern

The Leo Persona by Susanna Oroyan, breastplate construction for a 20" doll. Photo by W. Don Smith

Spellbinder by Gabriel Cyr and Sandy Blaylock, 23", fiber, leather, gourd, beads, twigs. Photo by Martin Fox

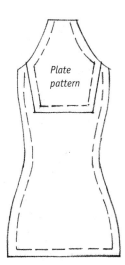

Plate pattern

Chest/neck pieces are drafted using the shoulder line of the basic torso pattern.

Cloth Breastplate Construction

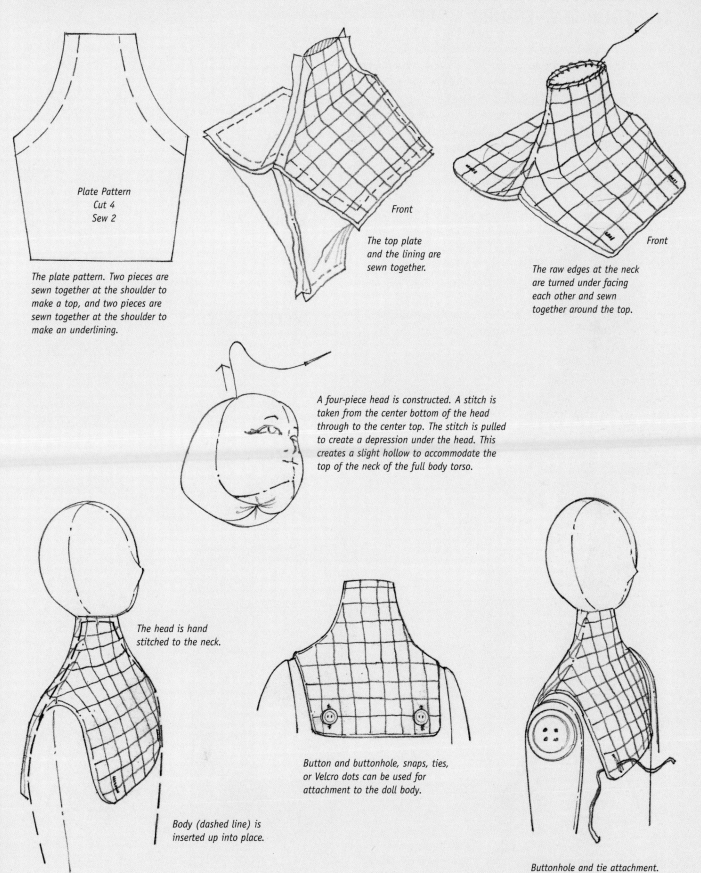

Plate Pattern
Cut 4
Sew 2

The plate pattern. Two pieces are sewn together at the shoulder to make a top, and two pieces are sewn together at the shoulder to make an underlining.

The top plate and the lining are sewn together.

Front

The raw edges at the neck are turned under facing each other and sewn together around the top.

Front

A four-piece head is constructed. A stitch is taken from the center bottom of the head through to the center top. The stitch is pulled to create a depression under the head. This creates a slight hollow to accommodate the top of the neck of the full body torso.

The head is hand stitched to the neck.

Button and buttonhole, snaps, ties, or Velcro dots can be used for attachment to the doll body.

Body (dashed line) is inserted up into place.

Buttonhole and tie attachment.

MULTIPLE PERSONALITIES: THE FOUR-WAY FIGURE

Many children and adults are enchanted by the discovery of another character hidden under the skirts of what looks to be "just a doll." Traditionally, these figures were two doll torsos sewn together and called topsy-turveys. At some point, a clever designer used the "add" word and decided there could be three figures, and thus the folktale characters "Little Red Riding Hood, Grandma, and the Wolf" could be made in one piece for story telling.

I applied the "add" word and decided that as there were four surfaces, there could certainly be four characters in a topsy-turvey piece. The result was Santa, Mrs. Santa, an Elf, and the Reindeer. There are any number of characters or character changes you can try. Antonette Cely used the simple topsy-turvey form to do the Virgin Mary in cloth.

Our Lady of the Painted Veil
by Antonette Cely, 18 ¹/₂",
paperclay over cloth.
Photos by Don Cely

Front   Body #1   Back

One doll head pattern is constructed so each side has a different character.
One doll pattern (your choice of design) is broken into two upper bodies.

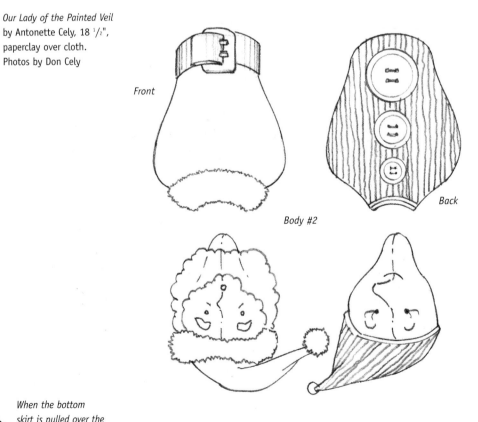

Front

Body #2   Back

When the bottom skirt is pulled over the head, a new figure in different colors is seen.

Reindeer side of four-way figure by Susanna Oroyan

Side view of heads. Mrs. Santa's cap is left loose at the back so it can be pulled over reindeer's antlers when she is presented.

Decide which dolls will go together and how they will be hidden.

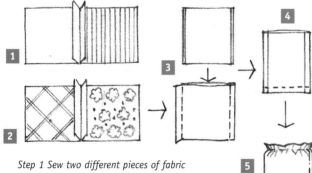

Step 1 Sew two different pieces of fabric together to make one skirt.

Step 2 Sew two different pieces of fabric together to make a second skirt (underskirt).

Step 3 Turn one skirt to right side out and slip it into second skirt.

Step 4 Sew skirts together at bottom.

Step 5 Pull skirts to right side and gather around raw edges at top.

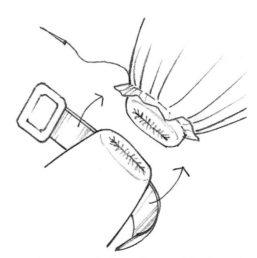

There are several ways to attach the two bodies and the skirt at the waist. On this doll, the two bodies were hand stitched together. Then the skirt was gathered to the waist of one torso, and the belt around the second torso hid the raw edges. Another way to attach the skirt might be to construct the skirt as above, except turn under the raw edges at top, and machine gather, leaving a finished ruffle at top. Slip the skirt over the torso and handstitch around the waist. One side will have a ruffled skirt top and the other will be plain gathers at the waist.

Another way to construct a four-way figure would be to construct one barbell shaped torso and give each end a head with two faces. Can you think of a better way?

CREATING A PATTERN FROM A SKETCH

Some people can create a doll form from a scrap of fabric, some can pick up scissors and cut a shape from cloth with no pattern, but more often than not dolls come from doodles. An artist will aimlessly play with pencil and paper until an interesting line or shape appears to suggest a character. In the case of the cowboys I had a headstart because I had to create a design to suit the woven fabrics.

The fabric suggested shirt and pants for the outdoors and the idea of cowboys. I drew the arc that became the shoulders and arms of "Shorty." Since the idea was to show the fabric, I did not want to break up the space with much seam detail so I only drew a line for the center front tummy curve. Now I could see the character of the cowboy who rides all day—short legs. Following the shoulder arc, the trouser outlines were penciled in. For comic contrast, I decided to use rather straight lines to make his tall, skinny pal. The drawings opposite are very close to the original sketches. Now I had to make the drawings into pattern shapes that could be sewn together to get the effect I wanted with dimension.

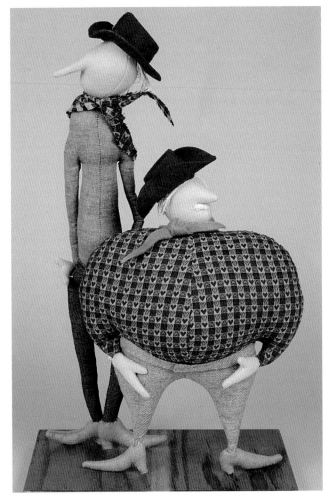

Shorty and Slim by Susanna Oroyan, 15" and 18", stuffed cloth.
Photo by W. Don Smith

I used a photocopier to enlarge the sketches to the approximate height I wanted. I made several copies at that size so I could cut out parts. My experience of what happens to fabric when it is sewn and stuffed now came into play. The stuffed part will always be smaller than the flat paper pattern piece so I had to add to the sketched parts to compensate. I also had to detail the trousers to allow for a little back-to-front depth, and this was done by adding a crotch curve. The shirt back pieces were curved slightly inward at the center back, but, as you can see, even with the adjustments, the pattern reproduced the same impact as the sketch when sewn up.

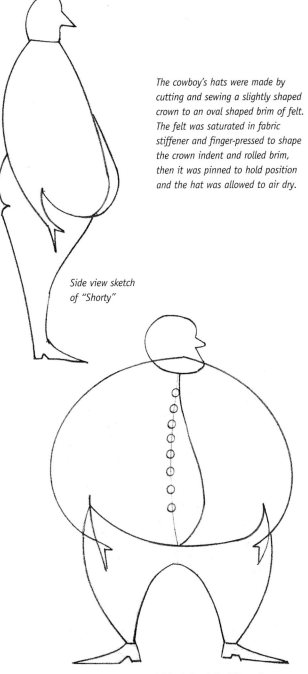

The cowboy's hats were made by cutting and sewing a slightly shaped crown to an oval shaped brim of felt. The felt was saturated in fabric stiffener and finger-pressed to shape the crown indent and rolled brim, then it was pinned to hold position and the hat was allowed to air dry.

Side view sketch of "Shorty"

Original sketch for "Shorty"

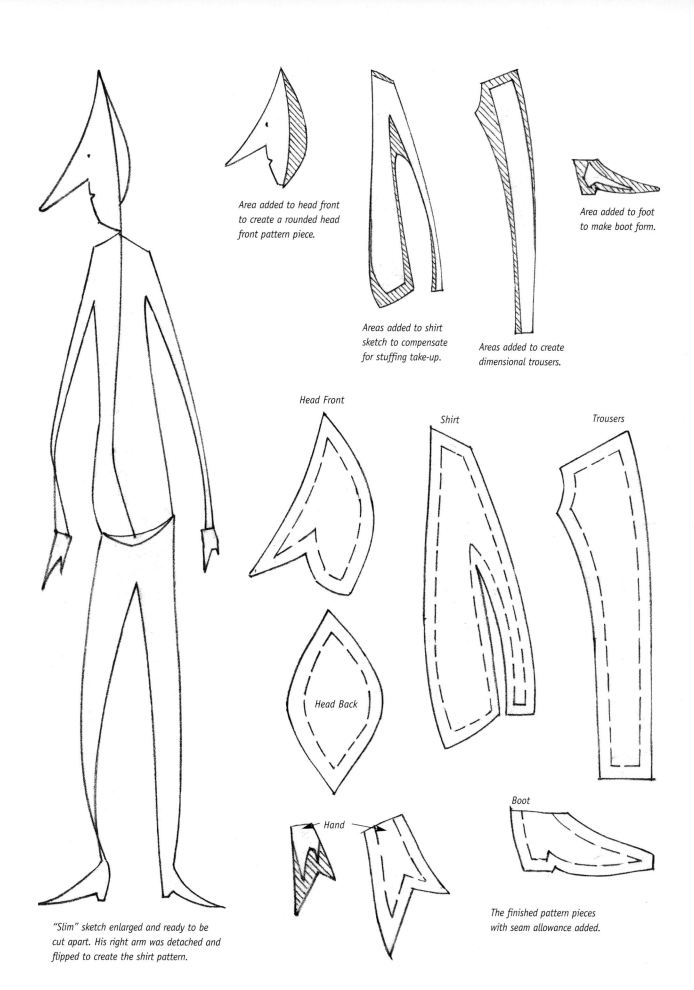

Area added to head front to create a rounded head front pattern piece.

Areas added to shirt sketch to compensate for stuffing take-up.

Areas added to create dimensional trousers.

Area added to foot to make boot form.

Head Front

Shirt

Trousers

Head Back

Hand

Boot

"Slim" sketch enlarged and ready to be cut apart. His right arm was detached and flipped to create the shirt pattern.

The finished pattern pieces with seam allowance added.

CLOTH NOTES

Bean Bags

The bean-bag or pellet-filled body is just plain fun to hold and play with. The shifting pellets can provide any number of amusing poses. All it takes is a simple form—don't do much in the way of darts because you want the pellets to make the shapes. Arms and legs can be attached. It is best to avoid organic fillers such as beans, rice, or birdseed as they attract animals and insects who might want to dine on them. You can find plastic pellets where doll supplies are sold, or you can try kitty litter.

Alternative Fillings

Some great effects might be achieved by combining unusual forms and fillings such as foam, Styrofoam, rubber shreds, or pellets (litter, sand, organic).

Skinning a Figure

Two-way stretch fabrics can be used to construct a body-suit for a figure. This can be used when you want to cover joints, seam lines, or a body made of a heavy material. Large bodies can be covered with stretch knit or velour, smaller ones with nylon stocking or tights materials. All you need to do is make a tube of the stretch material as wide as the narrowest area (ankle, wrist) and turn and pull it over the body part. If your figure has articulated fingers, sew hands separately from arms "sandwich style" with the finish fabric inside.

Yvette and Her Doll by Carole Bowling, 13" seated, cloth oil-painted over wire armature. Photo by Carole Bowling

Three Little Kittens by Susan Fosnot, 17", oil-painted cloth. Photo by CLIX Photographs and Savables

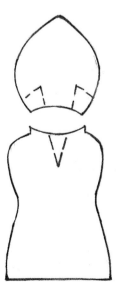

Pattern developed by Susan Fosnot with darts placed to provide both dimension and flat painting surface

Painting Grounds

Cheesecloth or tarlatan gauze stretched over a stuffed fabric figure provides a canvas-like ground for painting...will add to a brush-stroke effect.

Molded Faces

Be sure to sculpt enough chin for your mask. If you sculpt a neck, do the back as well for a nice finish. Some fabrics will allow you to pull excess to the back for stuffing. I think adding a head back makes it much more satisfactory for adding wig materials and finishing.

Machine Embroidery

Computerized sewing machines are now offering built-in stitch patterns for doll faces as well as the ability to scan in or program your own designs. The small-scale stitch patterns of a sewing machine offer wonderful opportunities for creating your own fabric trims and embellishments. When a print cannot be found in a small scale, a machine-stitched border or hemstitching might do the trick. I have used my machine to embroider gold thread patterns on leather for exotic shoes and fine embroidery details on doll lingerie. What can you do? If your machine has these capabilities, do consider how they can be used to good effect.

Stiffening

Fabric can be made hard by painting the surface or by soaking fabric in a stiffening material. The term for this is sizing. Common home products for sizing would be glue, paint, or laundry starch.

Commercial sizing products can be found in fabric and craft shops. Makers use sizing for stiffening face masks for molded heads, fixing hand/finger positions, modeling hat forms, giving permanent form to puffy areas like sleeves or large areas such as skirts. Most sizing materials are white and some will show in the fabric when dry. Always experiment with scrap fabrics to see what the effect will be.

Images on Fabric

In addition to painting, appliqué, and embroidery, there are many ways to produce an image or design on fabric using your computer, computer printers, typewriters, blueprint and photographic techniques. Jean Ray Laury's book, *Imagery on Fabric*, contains step-by-step procedures for many unusual techniques such as these.

Lateral Thinking

Designing for a "look" and designing for construction usually happen at the same time. This is where the artist moves from just creating decorated doll bodies to creating unique art figures.

Imagineering Is Communication

Repeat this: I want to make an idea in a form such that another person can share, at least part of, my thinking and experience. Making figures is one of the great ways in which we talk to each other about the human condition in general.

Japanese Bird by
Nancy Laverick, 22", cloth.
Photo by Nancy Laverick

Extrovert Pins
by Deb Shattil.
Photos by Deb Shattil

Learning to Critique

When I talked about attitude adjustment, I said that you had to take personal responsibility for making the piece. You also have to take responsibility for public reactions to the piece. If no one likes it, if no one buys it or awards it a ribbon, it must be lacking something. Whose fault is that? Yours because you made it. Do you care? Probably. You care because you love your piece and you want everyone else to appreciate it as much as you do. Critique is caring for work.

Critique should never be confused with anything negative, bad, or hurtful. Critique should be thought of as design evaluation. The words "look" and "see" are crucial. You look at your design and you see where it does not work to state your idea well. Remember, the brain will accept general concepts and fill in the blanks for you. Your job is to make your brain work a bit harder. Sometimes this means you have to give the brain a little more information to go on—other things to consider and relate to when it looks at the piece. You get this from education in all fields of dolls and doll-making, observation and analysis of other artists' work, and input from other people.

Input from other people comes in three ways: The judged competitive exhibit, the market, and formal critical comments from other artists whose work is considered to be successful.

Many people think winning a ribbon validates their work. Not necessarily. A ribbon means that you showed the right doll to the right people at the right time. A doll that wins a blue ribbon at the county fair show might not even place at a ceramic show. A doll that wins a ribbon at a ceramic show might not win at a show judged by doll artists working in several media. The value of a ribbon will depend totally on who you want to approve of your work. Judges are people with their own tastes and experiences that might not reflect what you do. Judges are not always artists themselves or design qualified. One judge can often sway the votes of a team. Sometimes dolls in competitions are ranked when all (or none) deserve a first.

On the other hand, you can learn immensely from a competition. You do the judging; you compare and pick apart the other entries; you teach yourself what things are good. If the judges are respected professionals, you will be able to see which dolls demonstrate more refined thought and technical application. These observations will give you some things to be aware of and work on improving.

Market input is purely a reflection of taste. It tells you what people will spend their money on or what things they consider investment/resale quality. These things might not equate to "good dolls." It probably means that the buyer likes angels and you had one at the right price. It can also mean that the shop owner who buys for resale knows what his customers will buy.

Direct input or comparative evaluation from respected artists is the best way to get valuable, usable input. You cannot do this by mail. No photo in the world will show details as the human eye can see them. You need to go to places where you can see work of other artists and where you can get first-hand critique. What this does for you is add another brain or two and more eyes to see.

Another artist critiquing will first try to see what your idea is and then weigh the elements of the piece against what you seem to want to communicate. He might say things like "This head is far too complex for such a simple costume, you need to consider simplifying your head or making more detailed costumes." He might say, "It looks like you are expressing joy, but all those brown tones don't underline that." He might say, "You have sculpted in a realistic mode, but these particular bones don't go in those places." He might say, as one said to me recently, "I like that piece but change the plastic centers in the silk flowers." That is a tiny thing, but a whole lot of tiny things keep your piece from adding up. Worse, it was a tiny thing that jarred someone else and kept them from fully appreciating the piece. I was lazy. Shame on me.

There is, of course, my taste. Maybe I really like plastic flower centers. If so, I must be able to point out why I can use them, why they work with other design elements. The doll in question was in period costume. There was no plastic in the era portrayed so I had no design defense. Additionally, the plastic looked "manufactured" against the natural look of the silk flowers. Poor choice of textures. If I can't defend my choice in design terms, I shouldn't use it even if I like it. It is always a question of what works for the piece. There should be a good reason for everything you use and choose. Happiness is when you can use things you like to make an effective piece.

Another observation often made in critiques is that the piece is not sure what it is supposed to be. Usually, this means that a maker has inserted a number of techniques and types that don't go with the subject. For instance, a highly detailed face on a soft play doll body with big bright print clothes, or joints on a costume figure or historical character, or a character face with highly detailed realistically scaled costume. Choose or invent a type and follow through in all treatments.

You are in trouble when your figures just "are" but don't "do" anything for the viewer. That means they lack power, are sterile. Remember that the artist's personality is in a work, but the emotion shown can be a reflection of something else in society that the artist may feel for, but not necessarily believe or have experienced. An artist is an interpreter and a teacher. Can your work help someone else to tell a story, to experience an emotion, or have a new perspective? Can it help him understand his emotions or the world around him? Those are the elements that create depth in a piece.

Not all dolls are meant to be power pieces. Some are meant to decorate sofas and beds, and some are meant to be played with. Even so, each one is a character or a little personality. Each one requires all the attention to design details—proportion, scale, form, line, pattern, texture, color—to make their personalities project.

Doing design evaluation critique for yourself involves being highly analytical. I find the best way is to describe the parts as thoroughly as possible and listen to what you say. For instance, if you describe the sole of the shoe as "black leather cut to equal ovals joined in the middle with a rough edge" key words will appear. Did you mean to have the front and the back of the sole equal? or do you want a more typical shape where the heel end is smaller? Can that rough edge be smoothed out? "The sleeve is gathered white satin." Are the gathers the same size as the gathers in your real-person clothes? If so, they are too big for the doll. Satin might be too heavy/large in scale to gather correctly. Maybe you need to find a satin-like finish in a lighter-weight fabric.

Following is a checklist for doing your own critique and for making comparative educational analysis of other work. These are based on the most common failings. Find them and fix them!

Each artist will tend to be aware of certain sets of things. For instance, one will see the curve of surface flesh in the fingers and make them round, others will be more aware of the bones and tendons and make more square fingers. This awareness and its consistent presentation is part of each artist's signature. The key word is consistency. Choose one point of view and stick to it all through the figure.

Each artist will tend to put his own anatomical features (or those of the nearest and dearest) into the artwork. But most of us aren't perfectly and uniformly well-designed. Use yourself for a reference, but be aware of the differences between your peculiarities and the design you want to communicate. Here are two examples: I have a lot of fat in my upper eyelid and when I smile, those heavy lids reduce my eye to little curved slits. This conformation might be all right for a character, but if I want to communicate a universal idea of beauty, I would have to take care to sculpt a nicely rounded open eye. A student of mine had a terrible time sculpting hands for a lady. Problem: she had a very advanced case of arthritis in her hands and she was copying her own anatomy.

Now, take a look at your piece in relation to the head checklist drawings (page 143). Find and fix any problems before curing and painting.

Critique Checklist

1. Is this a new idea, a new version of a traditional idea? What have I done differently?

2. Could this be mistaken for another artist's work style? How can I avoid this?

3. How do I want the viewer to react? What do I want him to think when he sees this piece? Who is this figure and what is it doing or telling? Have I made this clear?

4. Do the colors I have used enhance the idea? Do the prints and textures?

5. Is everything I have done in the same style? If realistic, all parts should be realistic and to exact scale.

6. Did the material choices blend well? Do I see figure and form first and fabric second? Do the fabrics look "off the bolt" or have I blended them in to my design? Can you identify the type of hair or does it look like it grew as a natural part of the doll?

7. Does the costume fit well? Is the sewing neat and tidy? Have I clipped thread ends, cleaned up glue runs?

8. Have I done a complete and clean job on the body surface? Is the sculpted surface cleaned and smooth? Is the painting neat?

9. Does this figure hold its pose? Stand up straight? Sit when placed? If it is on a stand, are its feet floating or on the ground? Have I made the costume look like gravity is affecting it correctly?

10. If there are accessories, do they fit well and look natural in the hands or do they just float on top of the fingers?

11. Have I used or made accessories in the right scale for the doll? Are they of the right material for the figure? Are there too many? Are they placed with thought to creating a whole "picture?"

12. Could I do with my body what I have done in the doll? (try it looking in a mirror)

13. Is this piece ready to go public or should I do another improved version?

Finished? Not yet. Turn your head upside down and look at its underneath cross section. Does it balance? Turn the head so you look up from the jaw up to the top of the head. Are both sides even?

Check and double-check yourself, learn to see how parts really work together dimensionally. Correct mistakes...no matter how long it takes. All the best artists will tell you that they continually work on "getting it right."

HANDS

If you poke around in artists' sketchbooks—da Vinci's for example—you will find drawing after drawing after drawing of hands. Why? They are the most fabulously engineered part of the anatomy—capable of technological and mechanical work as well as the most dramatic and graceful expression of emotion....and they are definitely deserving of the dollmaker's time and attention. Comic exaggeration or realistic rendition, they have to reflect a truly working body part.

In modeled figures, you can correct by addition and subtraction. In cloth figures, you correct by inserting wire armatures in the fingers, positioning stuffing, and bending so knuckle definition is suggested. In sewing the hand, you correct the ratio of roundness or fat palm by taking a dart at the thumb or inserting a separate thumb. If your design calls for it, you can define with needlesculpting to show muscle and tendon.

Note: the smaller the figure, the less small detail will show.

Freedom by Mary Worrow, 10", Fimo. Photo by Cassandra's Playmates

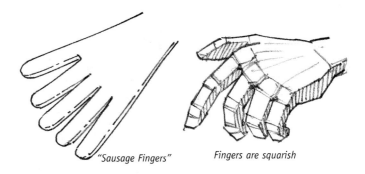

"Sausage Fingers"   Fingers are squarish

The biggest problems seen are usually "sausage fingers" or fingers that have no indication of knuckles (in the right place) or tendons.
In the first place, few fingers are round. Look at them, they are squarish.

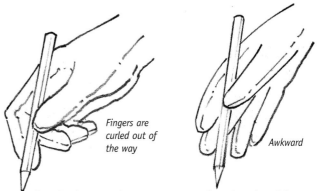

Fingers are curled out of the way   Awkward

See what happens when you move one—how the others follow. Notice what happens to the fingers not holding the pen or tool—all curled up and out of the way.

Fingers working in parallel   "V" space between fingers

Look again and move them. They work in parallel.

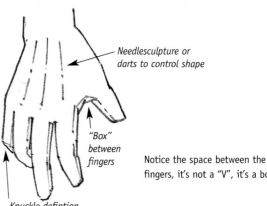

Needlesculpture or darts to control shape

"Box" between fingers

Knuckle defintion

Notice the space between the fingers, it's not a "V", it's a box.

QUICK CHECK CRITIQUE FOR HEADS

When we look at someone, we know their face has depth or dimension, although it appears to be flat. Most errors in sculpted heads are caused by the artist's drawing on clay rather than building up a skull covered with tissue. Learn to look at the sculpture from all angles equally.

1. The skull can be compared to an egg.

2. The jaw is a hinge on the egg.

3. The face is not flat. All parts fall back from the root of the nose.

4. The eye is a ball in a hole. The edge of that hole is the bone under the eyebrow line. Eyes should never protrude beyond that edge.

5. The eyes must track—both must look in the same direction.

6. The shape of the lid and eye muscle will change if the eyes have a sideways glance.

7. Painted eye highlights should be from behind or if figure looks forward be sure they are placed so highlight shows from one side on both eyes.

8. No matter how fat a person is or how much he smiles, there is always an indentation under the eye.

9. When a person smiles, the cheek muscles "gather" the skin backwards in a series of parallel lines.

10. Everyone has a line between the nose and corner of the mouth although it might not show on a fleshy or youthful face.

11. Everyone has a slight indentation below the corner of the lip.

12. The end of the nose almost never extends beyond a line to the inside corner of the eye.

13. The mouth is not a ring, it is a slit in the flesh. Lip width is added to the inside of the cut line.

14. Ears are placed on lines from the corner of the eye and just under the nose.... to keep your ears from floating up the head, be sure you hold head so that it is parallel to the ground and straight up and down.

15. The earlobe falls over the intersection of the jaw and back of skull.

16. The neck is straight. It never curves inwards.

17. And, lucky for us, it is rare we see all of both ears at once. However, what is seen must match.

18. Last but not least, problems are not always where they seem to be. For instance, if you just can't get the eye right, the problem could be that the top of the skull or forehead is not correct.

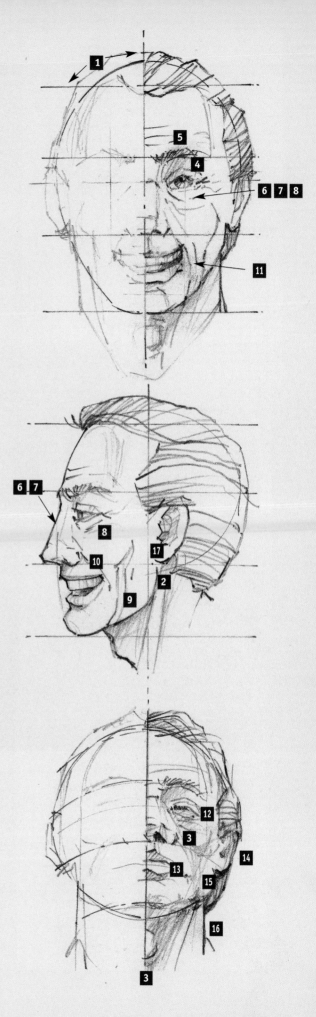

UPPER LEFT: *Keeper of the Keys* by Nancy Walters, 18",
porcelain, direct sculpture. Photo by Nancy Walters

UPPER RIGHT: *Angèle* by Jacques Dorier, 14", hand-painted
resin head, cloth body, paper hair and costume. Photo by
James Beards Photography

LOWER RIGHT: *Savannah* by Michele O'Neil, 20", Cernit.
Photo by G.R. Farley

UPPER LEFT: *I'm Tired and I Want to Go Gnome* by Jeanie Bates, 14"
seated, cloth needlesculpture. Photo by W.S. Sullivan

LOWER LEFT: *The Tea Party* by Jeanie Bates, 16", needlesculpted cloth.
Photo by W.S. Sullivan

UPPER RIGHT: *Fresh Catch* by Annie Wahl, 12", Super Sculpey. Photo by
W. Don Smith

TOP: *Flying Lessons* by Dorothy Allison Hoskins, 14" seated, porcelain, direct sculpture. Photo by W. Don Smith

UPPER LEFT: *Florentine Angel* by Rosemary Volpi, 21", polyform clay, paperclay over wire armature. Photo by Rosemary Volpi

LOWER LEFT: *Wynkyn, Blynken, and Nod* by Annie Wahl, 9-18", Super Sculpey. Photo by W. Don Smith

UPPER RIGHT: *Beth* by Diane Keeler, 12" seated, Cernit and Super Sculpey, cloth over wire armature body. Photo by Lloyd H. Wilson

UPPER LEFT: *The Pedicure* by Dorothy Allison Hoskins, 4¹/₂",
direct-sculpted porcelain. Photo by W. Don Smith

UPPER RIGHT: *Doll with Giraffe* by Marla Florio, 14", cloth.
Photo by Marla Florio

LOWER RIGHT: *Brooke* by Lorri Acott Fowler, 17", Fimo.
Photo by Lori Acott Fowler

UPPER LEFT: *Molly Can't Wait* by Jodi and Richard Creager, 10", Super Sculpey, wire and cloth torso. Photo by Richard Creager

LOWER LEFT: *Girl with Jester* by Carla Thompson, 26", felt molded over composition head and limbs, soft, posable body. Photo by Carla Thompson

UPPER RIGHT: *Young Dancer* by Carole Bowling, 20", Fimo and cloth over wire armature. Photo by Carole Bowling

UPPER LEFT: *Samantha* by Lynne Sward, 13", fabric, beads, machine and hand sewing. Photo by Michele Tillander/Atlantis

LOWER LEFT: *Into the Light of Day* by Olga Dvigoubsky Cinnamon, 12 1/2", cloth. Photo by Jeff D. Owen

UPPER RIGHT: *Laurel* by Lynne Sward, 15", cloth. Photo by Michelle Tillander/Atlantis

LOWER LEFT: *Goddess of the Beads* by Barbara Carleton Evans, 6", beadwork over felt core. Photo by Barbara Carleton Evans

UPPER RIGHT: *The Wise One* by Anne Mayer Meier, 36", clay, wood, fabric and leather. Photo by Jerry Anthony

UPPER LEFT: *Madame, Emilie and Annabelle After Practice* by Susanna Oroyan, 20", paperclay. Photo by W. Don Smith

LOWER LEFT: *Sun King* by John Darcy Noble, 12", paperclay over wire armature. Photo by Evan Bracken

PROTECTING YOURSELF/ RESPECTING OTHERS

What does copyright do? Publication of a work with the correct form of copyright notation is simply an announcement to the world that you have created the piece that has never been seen in that form before. The piece should be marked with the word "copyright" or the symbol "C" in a circle, or the letter c followed by a period, your name in full, and the date.

C. Jane Dollmaker, 1999

Copyright Jane Dollmaker, 1999

This marking is enough to publish copyright; however, for a nominal fee, you can register the work and receive a paper verification from the Copyright Office, Library of Congress, Washington, DC. Your library can help with forms or procedures for formal registration. For dolls, you would need to register it as a work of visual art.

The registration of copyright also states to the public that you have the rights of control over that work and its uses. There can be several possible uses. A doll could be manufactured, or its image photographed and used on a greeting card, or it could be used as a character in a movie. When you sell a doll, you can limit the rights of its usage. Very important for dollmakers, this means that others' work that is copyrighted (and we should always assume it is) is equally protected. For instance, you cannot make a doll that looks exactly like someone else's drawing or painting or photograph. The original illustrator or photographer probably holds a copyright on his drawing. If you want to reproduce it as a doll you need to get his written permission. Copyrights extend for many years so be sure to check on older, out-of-print works as well as current.

In order to copyright a work of art it must be your original concept. What you are protecting is your thinking, and that must be different from any other form in what is called "look and feel." Your doll should be different enough so a person would not confuse it with another's work in any way.

Many dollmakers work from purchased patterns. These can be copyrighted and/or patented. If a pattern is sold, the original creator grants the buyer some limited rights of reproduction. Usually, it means that you can make a limited number of dolls and sell them, but you cannot copy or reprint the pattern. If you make and sell dolls from the pattern, you must mark the tags so that the original designer or company gets proper credit. "Boopsy" an original design by Jane Dollmaker made by Betty Seamstress.

Technical process and the mechanics of a doll are not usually protected under copyright. A button joint is not protected as a joint, but might be protected if a unique button was used as part of its art statement. In most cases, the doll world considers technical process generic because it comes from the world of the art studio, classroom, and home sewing technique. Technical or mechanical process, if protected, is covered by patent. Like copyright, patents are registered in order to grant rights or license to reproduce. Patent life is of shorter duration and when not renewed becomes public property.

The main consideration with copyright and patent is to allow the artist/inventor the rights to make money on his thinking and creativity. If you want that for yourself, respect it in others' work.

Grandma's Ride by Jodi and Richard Creager, 16", Super Sculpey, wire and cloth torso. Photo by Richard Creager

STANDARD DEFINITIONS

The following is a summary of the Standard Definitions adopted by the National Institute of American Doll Artists, The British Doll Artist's Association, and the Original Doll Artist Council of America for their members. You might find them helpful in understanding, discussing or selling your work.

Artist-Designer

One who has an idea and transforms it into a three-dimensional doll by using his or her hands to sculpt or re-arrange raw materials.

The Idea

The starting point of the creation of any doll. The idea may be inspired by a story, an illustration, or a life experience of the artist, or it may be a concept given to an artist by an individual or manufacturer who is commissioning a piece. An artist using an idea directly inspired by an illustration, photograph, or individual needs to have written permission to reproduce the image from the individual or artist.

The Original or First Doll

The first doll is the object made by one artist who takes a lump of clay, a piece of wood, a length of fabric or other raw material and re-arranges it into a doll form which reflects a particular idea or concept. The work of the artist's hands and mind, the individual nature of the artist's approach to technical process, and the fact that this particular portrayal has never before been seen in three-dimensional reality makes the resulting work the first doll or the original.

One-of-a-Kind

When the original or first doll is sculpted, assembled, costumed, and finished by the artist and this is never made again, it is called a one-of-a-kind.

Design Prototype

If the original of the first doll is used for the purposes of reproduction, it becomes a design prototype. A design prototype may be used by the creating artist for production of his own editions, or it may be sold to a company for commercial reproduction.

Artist's Original Limited Series

Individual one-of-a-kind dolls handmade by the creating artist which form a "family" or related group because of shared similarities in costume, character, or theme. As each one is individually sculpted and constructed without a mold by the artist, they are essentially one-of-a-kind originals.

Limited Edition

When an original/design prototype is used to make molds and identical copies are reproduced from the molds in a predetermined number, the resulting group of dolls is called a limited edition. The amount to be made is advertised with the introduction of the doll. The molds will be broken at the completion of the specified number to guarantee the "rarity" of the edition.

Artist's Signature Edition

If the original/design prototype is used to make a mold and identical dolls are reproduced from the mold by the artist himself, the resulting dolls are called an artist's signature edition.

Artist's Limited Edition

If the artist has help with the construction (pouring, cleaning, costuming) of dolls made from his original molds, but does the majority of the work, maintaining full control over design and execution, the resulting dolls are called an artist's limited edition.

Artist's Studio Edition

Artist has control over production and quality, but all work is completed by staff.

Reproduction

A reproduction, or "copy of," is any doll made or produced by an individual or company from an existing mold or model, or pattern. In general, the term includes dolls made by artists from molds they make of their own original design prototypes. The more common usage of the term and its abbreviation "repro" refers to dolls made from purchased craft molds and sewing patterns, by makers who did not create the original design prototype. Making a mold and/or casting dolls from originals or molds, or copying patterns or selling dolls made from patterns without permission, is not acceptable. Copyrights may still be active even if the doll is unmarked or the original company is no longer in production. It is not acceptable to call any reproduction an original. Reproductions should always credit the creating artist as the original designer. Mold makers and some pattern makers give limited reproduction rights with purchase. If in doubt, check.

BOOKS AND MAGAZINES

Dollmaking is, by and large, a solitary occupation. Most people begin on their own, but when they find there are others out in the world who do what they do, they are eager to find out more. Accessible information comes from the magazines that can be delivered to your door for a few dollars a year. We suggest you sample the following periodicals and keep up to date with those which most fit your dollmaking interests.

Contemporary Doll Magazine,
Doll Crafter, and Soft Dolls and Animals Magazine
Scott Publications
30595 Eight Mile Road
Livonia, MI 48152

Dolls, the Collector's Magazine
Collector Communications
170 Fifth Avenue, 12th Floor
New York, New York 10010

The Cloth Doll
PO Box 2167
Lake Oswego, OR 97035

Doll Reader Magazine
6405 Flank Drive
Harrisburg, PA 17112

International Doll World
House of White Birches
306 East Parr Road
Berne, IN 46711

Association for People Who Like to Play with Dolls / Newsletter
1779 East Avenue
Hayward, CA 94541

No dollmaker can see or have too many books. However, when you look in a publisher's catalog or on the library shelves, you will find very few books—less than ten—that have been writen to specifically present the work of doll artists like those shown here. You will only be able to find a few books that directly deal with the technical aspects of dollmaking, and many of them will be out-of-print, or self-published by the artist, and impossible to find in a shop. The books and videotapes most likely to be of use to you will be ones the individual artists offer by direct mail. If you write to an artist for information, enclose a stamped envelope for return of catalog or purchasing information. They will appreciate it and it will guarantee you get a response. Always bear in mind that dollmaking involves technical processes from other areas—from working metal to making shoes. Look for your learning experience in those areas as well. And just look at anything that might be of interest with an open mind...you never know when some process, material, or effect from another field might be adaptable.

Alexander, Lyn, *Make Doll Shoes! Workbooks* (2 vols.), Cumberland, MD: Hobby House Press.
—Pattern Designing for Dressmakers

Arnold, Janet, *Patterns of Fashion*, 3 vols., London: MacMillan, 1982.

Bailey, Elinor Peace, *Mother Plays With Dolls*, McLean, VA: EPM, 1990.

Bradfield, Nancy. *Costume in Detail 1730-1930*, (3 vols.), London: Harrap, 1982.

Bullard, Helen, *The American Doll Artist*. Volume I, Boston: Charles T. Branford, 1965. Volume II, Kansas City, MO: Athena, 1975.

Cely, Antonette, *Creating Your Own Fabric*, SASE for price and ordering information to: 3592 Cherokee Rd., Atlanta, GA 30340

Davis, Charlene Roth, *Making Original Dolls of Composition, Bisque, and Porcelain*. New York, NY: Crown, 1980.

Edwards, Betty, *Drawing on the Right Side of the Brain*. Los Angeles, CA: J.P. Tracher, 1979.

Engeler, Marleen, *Sculpting Dolls in Cernit*. Livonia, MI: Scott, 1991.

Erickson, Rolf and Faith Wick, *Sculpting Little People* (2 vols.), Oneonta, NY: Seeley's Ceramic Service, 1988.

Faigen, Gary, *The Artist's Complete Guide to Facial Expressions*, New York, NY: Watson-Guptill, 1990.

Gautier, Dick, *The Art of Caricature*, New York, NY: Putnam, 1985.

Goddu, Krystyna and Wendy Lavitt, *The Doll by Contemporary Artists*, New York, NY: Abbreville, 1995.

Goodfellow, Caroline, *The Ultimate Doll Book*, New York, NY: Dorling Kindersley, 1993.

Grubbs, Daisy, *Modeling a Likeness in Clay: Step-by-Step Techniques for Capturing Character*, New York, NY: Watson-Guptill, 1982.

Gunzel, Hildegard, *Creating Original Porcelain Dolls*, Cumberland, MD: Hobby House Press, 1988.

Hamm, Jack, *Drawing the Head and Figure*, New York, NY: Grosset & Dunlap, 1967.

Hamm, Jack, *Cartooning the Head and Figure*. New York, NY: Grosset & Dunlap, 1963.

Holz, Loretta, *The How-To Book of International Dolls*, New York, NY: Crown, 1980.

Johl, Janet Pacter, *The Fascinating Story of Dolls*, Watkins Glen, NY: Century House, 1941, 1969.

Kato, Donna, *The Art of Polymer Clay*, New York, NY: Watson Guptill, 1997.

Kinzie, Sharon, *How to Paint Eyes*, Livonia, MI: Scott, 1989.

Laury, Jean Ray, *Dollmaking: A Creative Approach*, New York, NY: Von Nostrand Reinhold, 1970.

Lichtenfels, Lisa, *The Basic Head: Soft Sculpture Techniques*, 1991 PO Box 90537, Springfield, MA 01139

Liggett, John, *The Human Face*, New York, NY: Stein and Day, 1974.

Luccesi, Bruno, *Modeling the Head in Clay*, New York, NY: Watson-Guptill, 1979.

Margolis, Argie, ed. The Doll Source Book, Cincinnati, OH: Betterway Books, 1996

McFadden, Sybil, *Fawn Zeller's Porcelain Dollmaking Techniques*, Grantsville, MD: Hobby House Press, 1984.

McKinley, Robert, *Dollmaking: One Artist's Approach*, SASE for ordering information to: Nelson/McKinley Books 107 East Cary Street Richmond, VA 23219.

Miller, Richard McDermott, *Figure Sculpture in Wax and Plaster*, New York, NY:Watson-Guptil, 1971.

National Institute of American Doll Artists, *The Art of the Doll*, 1992, SASE for ordering information to: Barrie, Rt. 1, Box 9640 Loomis Hill Road, Waterbury Center, VT 05677.

Nunn, Joan, *Fashion in Costume 1200-1980*, London: Herbert 1984.

Oroyan, Susanna, *Dollmaker's Notebook, Working With Contracts*. Fabricat, 1993. *Dollmaker's Notebook. Competition and Critique*, 1993.

Oroyan, Susanna and Carol-Lynn Rossel Waugh, *Contemporary Artist Dolls. A Guide for the Collector*. Grantsville, MD: Hobby House Press, 1986.

Richter, Joachim, *Kunstlerpuppen*, (Vol. 1 and 2), Munich: Magica Lanterna Press, 1986, 1989.

Rixford, Ellen, *Three-Dimensional Illustration*, NewYork, NY: Watson-Guptil, 1992.

Robertson, Virginia, *How to Draw and Sculpt Cloth Doll Faces*, Overbrook, KA: Osage County Quilt Factory, 1996.

Roche, Nan, *The New Clays:Techniques and Approaches to Jewelry Making*, Rockville, MD: The Flower Valley Press, 1991.

Seeley, Mildred, *Judging Dolls*, Livonia, MI: Scott Publishing, 1991.

Schmahl, Marion, *Kunstobjekt Puppe*, 1989, Ravensburg, Germany: Weingarten, 1990. The Transition. Gelsenkirchen, Germany: Arachne, 1996.

Schrott, Rotraut, *Making Original and Portrait Dolls in Cernit*, Grantsville: Hobby House Press, 1993.

Schider, Frtiz, *An Atlas of Anatomy for Artists*, New York, NY: Dover ,1947, 1954.

St. George, Eleanor, *The Dolls of Yesterday*, New York, NY: Charles Scribner's Sons, 1948.

White, Gwen, *European and American Dolls*, London: Batsford, 1966.

Whelpley, Alice and Lee, *Doll Workshop*. (8 vols covering wax, mold making, composition, and costuming), Grantsville: Hobby House Press.

Winer, Mimi and Jim, *Mimi's New Clays for Dollmaking*, Point Pleasant, NJ, 1993. SASE for ordering information to: Books and Supplies, P.O. Box 662, Point Pleasant, NJ 08742.

BOOK DISTRIBUTORS

Write for catalog of titles available

Hobby House Press
1 Corporate Drive
Grantsville, MD 21536

Scott Publications
30595 Eight Mile Road
Livonia, MI 48152

SUPPLIERS

Casting Resin
Nick Hill
10 Cranberry Pines
Scarboro, ME 04074

Small Sculpture Tools
The Perfect Touch
24 Artesia
Conroe, TX 77304-2516

Sculpture House
100 Camp Meeting Avenue
Skillman, NJ 08558

Alumalite Casting Products
225 Parson Street
Kalamazoo, MI 49007

American Art Clay
4717 W. 16th Street
Indianapolis, IN 46222

Dollmaking Supplies
Osage County Quilt Factory
Box 490
Overbrook, KS 66524

Playhouse Imports
25377 Huntwood Ave.
Hayward, CA 94544

General Art Supplies
Sax Arts and Crafts
P.O. Box 2002
Milwaukee, WI 53021

General Supplies
One and Only Creations
P.O. Box 2730
68 Coombs, Suite N
Napa, CA 94559

Hair/Fibers
Fleece and Unicorn Doll Hair Company
720 S. Husband St. Suite 4
Stillwater, OK 74074

Hand Turning Tools
Jackie Casey
Rt 2, Box 405
Murphey, NC 28906

MagicSculpt
3239 Monier Circle, Suite 5
Rancho Cordova, CA 95742

Mohair
So Susie Spins
6641 Sparta Road
Fredericktown, OH 43019

Paperclay
Creative Paperclay
1800 S. Robertson Blvd.
Los Angeles, CA 90035

Patterns
Timberpond Press
1133 West Broad Street
Williamstown, PA 17098

Photography
Smith Studios
624 N.E. 62nd Avenue
Portland, OR 97213

Sculpey, Polyform Clays
Polyform Products
1901 Estes Ave.
Elk Grove Village, IL 60007

Tools, Trims, Notions
All My Own
9695 63rd Ave. N.
Maple Grove, MN 55369

Wax
Walnut Hill Enterprises
P.O. Box 599
Bristol, PA 19007

LIST OF ARTISTS

1. Akune, Chikako, 5-25-9 Soshigaya, Setagaya-ku, Tokyo, Japan 157-0072
2. Angelique, Lawan, 2458 West Bayshore Road #7, Palo Alto, CA 94303
3. Anzai, Akiko, 1609 Treehouse Lane, Roanoke, TX 76262
4. Armas, Pamela, 3435 Texas Street, San Diego, CA 92104
5. Austin, Sara, 4035 Stalwart Drive, Rancho Palos Verdes, CA 90275
6. Bailey, Elinor Peace, 1779 East Avenue, Hayward, CA 94541
7. Baker, Betsey, ODACA, RR 2 Box 87, Hy-Vue Terrace, Cold Spring, NY 10516
8. Bates, Jeannie, 8957 S.W. Arapaho Road, Tualatin, OR 97062
9. Batte, Charles NIADA, 272 Divisadero St., #4. San Francisco, CA 94117
10. Baumbauer, Diana S., 1716 Melbourne Road, Lafayette, IN 47904
11. Beacock, Donna, 1146 Inglewood Road, Hayward, CA 94544
12. Wylde-Beem, Annie, 2943 Apache Avenue, Ventura, CA 93001
13. Bell, Floyd, NIADA, 10644 S. Wilton Place, Los Angeles, CA 90047
14. Bibb, Pattie 247 Overlook Drive, Chuluota, FL 32766
15. Boers, Martha and Marianne Reitsma, 1890 Parkside Drive, Pickering,ONT, Cananda, LIV3S4
16. Bowling, Carole, NIADA, 960 Quail Hollow Drive, Hollister, CA 95023
17. Brandon, Elizabeth, NIADA - address withheld
18. Brauser, Uta, 195 Chrystie Street, #203, New York, NY 10002
19. Cadiou, Karen, 3381 River Road, Terry, OH 44081
20. Calhoun, Lynne A. and Debbi McCullough, 4430 N. Rockcliff Place, Tucson, AZ 85750
21. Cannon, Marjory, 910 Donner Way, #204, Salt Lake City, UT 84108
22. Carlin, Caty, Route 2, Box 1077, Burnsville, NC 28714
23. Carroll, Toni , 491 Blackwood Drive, Longwood, FL 32750
24. Casey, Jacqueline, Route 2 Box 405, Murphy, NC 28906
25. Cely, Antonette, NIADA, 3592 Cherokee Road, Atlanta, GA 30340
26. Chapman, Barbara, 353 Glenmont Drive, Solano Beach, CA 92075
27. Charleson, Gillie, ODACA, 8 Belton Road, Adlington, Near Chorley, Lancashire, PP69NA England
28. Chomik, Chris and Peter Meder, NIADA, 5248 52nd Avenue North, St. Petersburg, FL 33709
29. Cinnamon, Olga Dvigoubsky, 1158 W/ 23rd Street, Upland, CA 91784
30. Clarke, Kathi, ODACA140 Jackson, Oconto, WI 54153
31. Creager, Jodi and Richard, NIADA 14704 B Gold Creek Court, Grass Valley, CA 95949
32. Cumming, Delores, 15 Sloop Lane, Berlin, MD 21811
33. Cunningham, Robert, 40 McGee Ave, #510, Kitchener, ONT, Canada N2B 2T3
34. Cyr, Gabriel and Sandy Blaylock, 291 East Chestnut, Asheville, NC 28801
35. Darin, Jane, 4757 Edison Street, San Diego, CA 92117
36. Davies, Jane, Amber NIADA, The Street, Walburton, Arundel, Sussex, England BNI8 0PH
37. Dorier, Jacques, 93 Shirley Street, Winthrop, MA 02152
38. Doucette, Robert, 12846 Woodbridge Street, Studio City, CA 91604
39. Draugalis, Marian, 805 W. Huron, Ann Arbor, MI 48103
40. Dunham, Susan, 36429 Row River Road, Cottage Grove, OR 97424
41. Dupont, Marie-Claude, 3798 Avenue Northcliffe, Montreal, Quebec, Canada H4A 3L1
42. Tolido-Elzer, Lillian, NIADA, Clavecimbellan 333, 2287 VM, Rijswyk, Netherlands
43. Easter, Lorna, 396 Brookedale Ct., Vacaville CA 95687
44. Engeler, Marlene, Noordeinde 67, 1141 AH Monnickendam, The Netherlands
45. Esslinger, Dru, R#2, Box 630, Madison, KS 66860
46. Evans, Barbara Carleton, 124 Poli Street, Ventura, CA 93001
47. Feingold, Sandra L., 1752 Gascony Road, Encinitas, CA 92024
48. Florio, Marla, 24514 Sarah Flynn Court, Novi, MI 48374
49. Flueler-Tomamichel, Elizabeth, NIADA, Bodenacherstrasse, 87, CH-8121 Benglen, ZH, Switzerland
50. Foley, Robin, 2917 S.W. Fairview Blvd, Portland, OR 97201
51. Fosnot, Susan, 322 South Madison Street, Woodstock, IL 60098
52. Fowler, Lorri Acott, 1602 Charleston Way, Fort Collins, CO 80526
53. Frank, Mary Ellen, NIADA, P.O. Box 021137, Juneau, AK, 99802
54. Gelin, Joanne, 120 Woodland Drive, Huntington, WV 25705
55. Goodnow, June, NIADA, 2324 Ashley Drive, Oklahoma City, OK 73120
56. Gray, Scott, NIADA 1101 17th Avenue, #308, Seattle, WA 98122
57. Hamilton, Jill N. 1481 Cranberry Court, Wixom, MI 48393
58. Hand, Martha, NIADA, 575 Worcester Ave, Cambria, CA 93428, 60.
59. Hanslik, Retagene, 533 Fairview Avenue, Arcadia, CA 91007
60. Harper, Elizabeth, 1830 N. Jameson Lane, Santa Barbara, CA 93108
61. Hart, Marcie, HC33, Box 3218 Boise, ID 83706
62. Hastings, Pamela, 161 Wilhelm Road, Saugerties, NY 12977

63. Hayes, Bronwyn, 18 Molineaux Place, Farrer, A.C.T. 2607. AUSTRALIA
64. Hoskins, Dorothy Allison, NIADA, 1411 Mary Ann, Fairbanks, AK 99701
65. Justiss, Sandra Wright, ODACA 720 Maplewood Avenue, Ambridge, PA 15003
66. Karaby, Adnan, deceased.
67. Katin, Hedy, ODACA 8 Palm Drive, Yankeetown, FL 34498
68. Keeler, Diane, 1972 300th Avenue, Luck, WI 54853
69. Kingman, Barbara, 2108 Meadow Lane, Topeka, KS 66614
70. Klawitter, Judith, 2303 River Road, Missoula, MT 59801
71. Koffrie, Henne, NIADA, Gen. K.v.d. Heydenlaan 9a, 3743 KT Baarn, The Netherlands
72. Lackman, Kate, 6573 Westover Circle, Cincinnati, OH 45236
73. Lampi, Sally, 2261 Beckham Way, Hayward, CA 94541
74. Laverick, Nancy, 6517-D, Four Winds Drive, Charlotte, NC 28212
75. Liesfeld, Junko, 12346 Casco Mill Lane, Montpelier, VA 23192
76. Lichtenfels, Lisa, NIADA, Box 90537, Springfield, MA 01139
77. Libby, Erin, 211 Hawthorn Road, Bellingham, WA 98225
78. Maciak, Heather, NIADA, 387 Glamorgan Circle, SW, Calgary, AB, Canada, T3E 5B7
79. Mason, Penny S., 10140 Gibbs, Clarkston, MI 48348
80. Matsubara, Toyoko, 12346 Casco Mill Lane, Montpelier, VA 23192
81. Mayer, Maggie, 4116 Michigan Shores Drive, Menominee, MI 49858
82. Meier, Anne Mayer, 124 Broadmoor Drive, Daphnne, AL 36526
83. Nelson, Bill, NIADA, 107 East Cary Street, Richmond, VA 23219
84. Newcombe, Thea, 3074 Country Drive, Eugene, OR 97401
85. Noble, John Darcy, 615 Hutchison Street, Vista, CA 92074
86. Oglesby, Sandra Thomas, 1160 Glenwood Trail, Deland, FL 32720
87. O'Neil, Michele, 9475 Jaclyn Avenue, Sauquoit, NY 13456
88. Oroyan, Susanna , NIADA, 3270 Whitbeck Boulevard, Eugene, OR 97405
89. Ouren, Janet Louise, 2414 Pleasant Creek, Kingwood, TX 77345
90. Owen, Emily, 145 Irish Settlement Road, Colton, NY 13625
91. Primozic, Lizzie Oz, 57 Taft Avenue, Providence, RI 02906
92. Radefeld, Beverly Dodge, 10650 N.W. 13th, Topeka, KS 66615
93. Rasmussen, Gerda, 1227 Sunset Cliffs Blvd, San Diego, CA 92107
94. Reiter, Lawrence, 1835 Myrtle Avenue, San Diego, CA 92103
95. Cowart-Rickman, Pamela, NIADA, P.O. Box 602 Rock Hall, MD 21661
96. Rixford, Ellen, 308 W 97th St., #71, New York, NY 10025
97. Robertson, Virginia , Box 490, Overbrook, KS 66524
98. Roche, Lynne and Michael, NIADA, 2 Lansdown Terrace, Lansdown Road, Bath, England,. BA1 5EF
99. St. Clair, Richard, 1626 Naudain St., Philadelphia, PA 19146
100. Sasaki, Akiko, 3-5-14 Kamiichi, Kashiwara-shi, Osaka, Japan 582
101. Schneider, Karan, 339 Trunbull Drive, Niles, OH 44446
102. Shattil, Deb, 9200 Skyline Blvd, Oakland, CA 94611
103. Shaw, Elizabeth, PO Box 223, Otisville, MI 48463
104. Skeen, Janet Kay, 10182 Quivas Street, Thornton, CO 80221
105. Smith, Connie, NIADA, 167 Gayle Avenue, Galatin, TN 37066
106. Stanley, Carroll, 223 Woodlyn Ave, Glenside, PA 19038
107. Stern, Andrea, 44 Ellis Ave, Chauncey, OH 45719
108. Stuart, George, NIADA, P.O.Box 508, Ojai, CA 93024
109. Stygles, Carol, 3375 Hoyer Road, Jackson, MI 49201
110. Sward, Lynne, 625 Bishop Drive, Virginia Beach, VA 23455
111. Talbot, Angela, 57 Martinridge Crescent, N.E. Calgary, Alberta, Canada, T3J 3MY
112. Thomas, Mary, 122 Brookside Place, Marina, CA 93933
113. Thompson, Carla, NIADA, 2002 Roundleaf Green, Huntsville, AL 35803
114. Thompson, Jolene, 8605 N.E. Milton, Portland, OR 9722
115. Trilling, Jo Ellen, NIADA, 43 E. 60th A-62 New York, NY 10022
116. Triplett, Dee Dee, 10286 Highway 19 West, Bryson City, NC 28713
117. van der Spiegel, Willemijn, Paardenmarkt 8, Doesburg, 6981 al, Netherlands
118. Volpi, Rosemary, 4580 Sheri Lyn Court, Los Vegas, NV 89121
119. Von Essen, Kenneth, NIADA, 306 Emerald, Redondo Beach, CA 90277
120. Wahl, Annie, NIADA, 22275 Penn Avenue, Lakeville, MN 55044
121. Walmsley, Katherine, NIADA, 8041 Shady Road, Oldenburg, IN
122. Walters, Nancy, NIADA, 690 Trinity Court, Longwood, FL 32750
123. Welch, Marcella, 5475 Route 93, Andover, OH 44003
124. Wickstrom, Amy, 400 Linda Lane, Opelousas, LA 70570
125. Wiley, Nancy, NIADA, 253 Warren Street, Hudson NY 12534
126. Worrow, Mary-Annette, 1116 New Jersey Ave., Altamonti Springs, FL 32714

INDEX

Knettie and Purlie Together by Connie Smith, 16" seated, direct-sculpted porcelain, fabric, mixed media. Photo by Connie Smith

ABOUT THE AUTHOR

Susanna Oroyan taught herself the art of dollmaking. Since 1972, she has made over 500 dolls, and her dollmaking has become a full-time career and business. For the past decade, Susanna has been a motivating force in regional and national dollmakers' organizations. She has exhibited her dolls internationally, and in 1995 received the Dollmaker of the Year award at the National Cloth Doll Festival. Susanna is the author of *Fantastic Figures* and *Anatomy of a Doll*, and has written numerous articles for doll magazines. She has also taught dollmaking classes at many major seminars as well as for individual dollmaking groups. Susanna's cloth-doll patterns are available from:

Fabricat Designs
3270 Whitbeck Boulevard
Eugene, OR 97405

Other Fine Books From C&T Publishing:

Anatomy of a Doll: The Fabric Sculptor's Handbook, Susanna Oroyan
Appliqué 12 Easy Ways! Elly Sienkiewicz
Art & Inspirations: Ruth B. McDowell, Ruth B. McDowell
The Art of Silk Ribbon Embroidery, Judith Baker Montano
The Artful Ribbon, Candace Kling
Buttonhole Stitch Appliqué, Jean Wells
A Colorful Book, Yvonne Porcella
Colors Changing Hue, Yvonne Porcella
Crazy Quilt Handbook, Judith Montano
Crazy Quilt Odyssey, Judith Montano
Curves in Motion: Quilt Designs & Techniques, Judy B. Dales
Deidre Scherer: Work in Fabric & Thread, Deidre Scherer
Dimensional Appliqué: Baskets, Blooms & Baltimore Borders, Elly Sienkiewicz
Easy Pieces: Creative Color Play with Two Simple Blocks, Margaret Miller
Elegant Stitches: An Illustrated Stitch Guide & Source Book of Inspiration, Judith Baker Montano
Everything Flowers: Quilts from the Garden, Jean and Valori Wells
The Fabric Makes the Quilt, Roberta Horton
Faces & Places: Images in Appliqué, Charlotte Warr Andersen
Fantastic Figures: Ideas & Techniques Using the New Clays, Susanna Oroyan
Focus on Features: Life-like Portrayals in Appliqué, Charlotte Warr Andersen
Free Stuff for Quilters on the Internet, Judy Heim and Gloria Hansen
From Fiber to Fabric: The Essential Guide to Quiltmaking Textiles, Harriet Hargrave
Heirloom Machine Quilting, Third Edition, Harriet Hargrave
Imagery on Fabric, Second Edition, Jean Ray Laury
Judith B. Montano: Art & Inspirations, Judith B. Montano
Mastering Machine Appliqué, Harriet Hargrave
On the Surface:Thread Embellishment & Fabric Manipulation, Wendy Hill
Papercuts and Plenty, Vol. III of Baltimore Beauties and Beyond, Elly Sienkiewicz
Pieced Clothing Variations, Yvonne Porcella
Quilts, Quilts, and More Quilts! Diana McClun and Laura Nownes
Recollections, Judith Baker Montano
RIVA: If Ya Wanna Look Good Honey, Your Feet Gotta Hurt...,Ruth Reynolds
Six Color World: Color, Cloth, Quilts & Wearables, Yvonne Porcella
Yvonne Porcella: Art & Inspirations, Yvonne Porcella

For more information write for a free catalog:
C&T Publishing, Inc.
P.O. Box 1456
Lafayette, CA 94549
(800) 284-1114
http://www.ctpub.com
e-mail: ctinfo@ctpub.com

For quilting supplies:
Cotton Patch Mail Order
3405 Hall Lane, Dept. CTB
Lafayette, CA 94549
e-mail: cottonpa@aol.com
(800) 835-4418
(925) 283-7883